BASICS OF NEUROREHABILITATION

For patients, families, and medical professionals

Erkinbek Dzhamanbaev (Dr.Erkin)

Basics of neurorehabilitation

Basics of neuro rehabilitation
For patients, families, and medical professionals

Authors:

- **Dr.Erkin (Dzhamanbaev)** – Medical Director of the International Neuro rehabilitation Center Adeli (Slovakia), Doctor of Medicine. Doctor of Internal Medicine, Anesthesiologist, Pain Management Doctor, Disaster Medicine Doctor, Doctor of Ayurveda and Yoga Therapy.
- **Dr. Diana Pohilko** – Licensed Mental Health Counselor, Psychotherapist, Gestalt Therapist and supervisor Trainer in Gestalt Therapy.
- **M.Sc. Katarina Bolerazska**, Licensed Speech Therapist.

This book includes several major parts:

1. Modern concept of the neurorehabilitation
2. Classifications and definitions of the neurological diseases
3. Some important and less known anatomical structures important in the neuro rehabilitation process
4. The most common causes leading to the neurological problems
5. Rehabilitation methods used in the world (most commonly)
6. Psychological aspects in the neurorehabilitation
7. Understanding speech therapy

The book is written for the patients, their families and practicing n=medical professionals who are interested in the questions of rehabilitation.

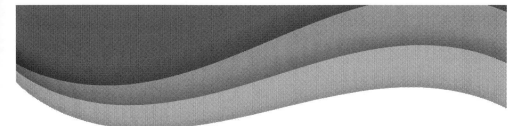

Contents

PART I

WHAT IS MODERN REHABILITATION CONCEPT?

DISABILITY AND REHABILITATION

Many neurological disorders and conditions affect an individual's functioning and result in disabilities or limit activities and restrict participation. According to the International Classification of Functioning, Disability, and Health (ICF), the medical model views disability as a person's problem, directly caused by disease, trauma, or other health conditions that require medical care in the form of individual treatment.

Management of the disability is aimed at cure or the individual's adjustment and behavior change. The social model of disability sees the issue mainly as a socially created problem and a matter related to individuals' full integration into society.

Rehabilitation

WHO defines rehabilitation as an active process by which those affected by injury or disease achieve a full recovery or, if a full recovery is not possible, realize their optimal physical, mental and social potential and are integrated into their most appropriate environment. Rehabilitation is one of the critical components of the primary healthcare strategy and the promotion, prevention, and treatment. While advertising and prevention primarily target risk factors of disease and treatment targets ill-health, rehabilitation targets human functioning. As with other key health strategies, it is of varying importance and is relevant to all other medical specialties and health professions.

Rehabilitation aims to enable people who experience or are at risk of disability to achieve optimal functioning, autonomy, and self-determination in the interaction with the more extensive physical, social, and economic environment. It is based on the integrative model of human functioning, disability, and health, which understands human functioning and disability both as an experience in relation to health conditions and impairments and interaction with the environment. Rehabilitation involves a collaborative and iterative problem-solving process along the continuum of care from the acute hospital to the community.

It is based on four fundamental approaches integrating a broad spectrum of interventions:

1) biomedical and engineering approaches;
2) build on and strengthen the resources of the person;
3) provide for a facilitating environment;
4) guide services, sectors, and payers.

Specific rehabilitation interventions include physical medicine, pharmacology and nutrition, psychology and behavior, education and counseling, occupational and vocational advice, social and supportive services, architecture and engineering, and other interventions. Rehabilitation services

What is rehabilitation:
- Prevention of the loss of function
- Slowing the rate of loss of function
- Improvement or restoration of function
- Compensation for lost function
- Maintenance of current function

are like bridges between isolation and exclusion — often the first step towards achieving fundamental rights. Health is a fundamental right, and rehabilitation is a powerful tool to provide personal empowerment.

The iterative problem-solving process is called Rehab-CYCLE. The Rehab-CYCLE involves four steps: assess, assign, intervene, and evaluate. The process is applied on two levels. The first refers to the guidance along the continuum of care, and the second to provide a specific service.

1. The **assessment** step includes identifying the person's problems and needs, evaluating rehabilitation potential and prognosis, and the definition of long-term service and goals of the intervention program.

The assignment step refers to the assignment to a service and an intervention program. From the guidance perspective, the intervention step is not further specified.

2. The **evaluation** step refers to service and the achievement of the intervention goal. From the service perspective, the assessment step includes identifying a person's problems, the review and potential modification of the intervention program's service or goals, and the definition of the first Rehab-CYCLE goals and intervention targets.

3. The **intervention** step refers to the intervention techniques' specification, the definition of indicator measures to follow the intervention's progress, and target values' definition to be achieved within a predetermined period.

4. The **evaluation** step refers to evaluating the goal's achievement concerning the specified target values of the indicator measures, the Rehab-CYCLE goals, and ultimately the intervention program's goals. It also includes the decision regarding the need for another intervention cycle based on a reassessment.

Rehabilitation of neurological disorders.

Rehabilitation should start as soon as possible after diagnosing a neurological disorder or condition and should focus on the community rehabilitation perspective. Rehabilitation is often exclusively associated with well-established and coordinated multidisciplinary efforts by specialized rehabilitation services. While availability and access to these specialized inpatient or outpatient services are at the core of successful rehabilitation, a need exists for rehabilitation service provision. From the acute settings through the district hospital and the community, health professionals are often not specialized in rehabilitation but work closely with the rehabilitation professionals. It is essential to recognize that rehabilitation efforts in the community can be delivered by professionals outside the health sector, ideally in collaboration with rehabilitation professionals.

The philosophy of rehabilitation emphasizes patient education and self-management and is well suited for some neurological conditions. The basis for successful neurorehabilitation is the in-depth understanding and measurement of functioning and the application of effective interventions, intervention programs, and services. A wide range of rehabilitation interventions, intervention programs, and services has been shown to contribute effectively to people's optimal functioning with neurological conditions. Effective neurorehabilitation is based on expert and multidisciplinary assessment, realistic and goal-oriented programs, and evaluation of the impact on the patient's rehabilitation achievements; evaluation using scientifically sound and clinically appropriate outcome measures should also incorporate the patient's and the family's perspectives.

There are several complexities in the process of neurorehabilitation, as patients can present with diverse sequelae, including the following:

Physical functioning limitations can be evident in many ways — such as paralysis of the body or its sides — limiting the person's capacity for many daily living activities and mobility in the community and, eventually, the capacity to return to work school. Patients can also present with rigidity, uncoordinated movements, and weakness.

People with disabilities have minimal access to rehabilitation services and appropriate assistive technology, such as adequate wheelchairs. Persons with a head injury who require wheelchairs for adequate positioning and mobility may be severely impaired in their possibility to leave their house and participate in community activities, access educational facilities, or work.

Cognitive impairments can manifest in memory and attention problems, mild to severe intellectual deficiency, lack of perseverance, and a limited ability to learn. These can make it impossible to return to work, affect emotional stability, and limit performance at work or home. All of these problems will affect a person's emotional status and that of the family and friends. It can also mean social isolation in the long term, aggravating depression.

Behavioral problems such as poor impulse control, uncontrolled anger and sexual impulses, lack of insight and perseverance, and the impossibility to learn from past errors are only some of the behavioral sequelae that affect the person's capacity to get involved. And this to be accepted socially and further limit the possibility of returning to educational or vocational services. Behavioral problems can also become evident when the person affected realizes the severity of their limitations and the fact that they may be permanent. Communication impairments in the form of speech problems, poor vocalization, or stomas, combined with lack of access to augmentative or alternative communication devices, are a sure means of social isolation.

Necessary daily living activities are affected by functional and cognitive limitations. Such things as getting dressed or getting a spoonful of food to his mouth can be impossible. Psychosocial constraints, such as limited access to education, the impossibility of returning to vocational status or being relocated vocationally, are consequences of previously mentioned limitations. These further impact the person's behavioral, physical, and cognitive aspects affected by a neurological disorder that causes disability.

PRINCIPLES OF NEUROLOGICAL REHABILITATION

Neurological rehabilitation is in many ways different from the other branches of neurology. **Rehabilitation is a process of education of the disabled person with the ultimate aim of assisting that individual to cope with family, friends, work, and leisure as independently as possible**. It is a process that centrally involves the disabled person in making plans and setting essential and relevant goals to their particular circumstances. In other words, it is a process that is not done to the disabled person but a process that is done by the disabled person themselves, but with the guidance, support, and help of a wide range of professionals.

Rehabilitation has to go beyond the relatively narrow confines of physical disease and needs to deal with the psychological consequences of disability and the social milieu in which the disabled person has to function. Thus, a key factor that differentiates rehabilitation from much of neurology is that it is not a process that neurologists can carry out alone but requires an active partnership with a whole range of health and social service professionals.

The rehabilitation process
- An educational process
- Central involvement of the disabled person in program planning
- Key involvement of family, friends, and colleagues
- A process that requires clear goals to be set and measured
- An interdisciplinary process
- A process based on the concepts of disability (activity) and handicap (participation)

Because of the complexity of rehabilitation based on the above-mentioned integrative model, rehabilitation services and interventions applying the rehabilitation strategy need to be coordinated along the continuum of care across specialized and non-specialized services, sectors, and payers.

IMPAIRMENT, DISABILITY, AND HANDICAP

These are key concepts that form the basic principles of neurological rehabilitation. The concepts were developed by the World Health Organization in 1980. Although the terms have recently been modernized (and the new definitions are discussed below), the three original terms—impairment, disability, and handicap—are so well known and so ingrained in the philosophy of neurological rehabilitation that it is worthwhile discussing the older terms in the first instance. **Impairment is just a descriptive term. It implies nothing about consequence.**

Examples are right hemiparesis, left-sided sensory loss, or homonymous hemianopia.

However, a right hemiparesis can obviously be relatively mild and lead to virtually no functional consequence or severe and lead to a complete inability to walk. **The functional consequence of impairment is a disability.** Investigative and diagnostic neurology clearly needs to identify the impairment in order to lead to appropriate investigations and eventual diagnosis. **However, neurological rehabilitation goes beyond the impairment and looks at the functional consequence, and tries to minimize the impact of the disability on the individual.**

Thus, neurological rehabilitation mainly deals with disability. However, the concept of handicap is equally important. **Handicap is the description of the social context of the disability.** A person with right hemiparesis, for example, may have a relatively mild weakness, but even a limited weakness may have profound social consequences for some people. A young man with such hemiparesis may, for example, wish to go into the armed forces or be a long-distance lorry driver, and both occupations would be closed to him, or an existing job may be lost. However, an older man with a similar hemiparesis degree may have virtually no limitations placed on his lifestyle.

Thus, handicap looks beyond the disability into the broader social context, which will often have implications for the rehabilitation process's goals.

Neurological rehabilitation needs to take into account not only the disability but also the particular handicap for the individual while bearing in mind that some of the social and physical barriers depend on societal attitudes and the physical environment and may be outside the control of the rehabilitation team. Recently the WHO has produced a new classification, which has fewer negative connotations.

Disability is now termed activity, and handicap is now termed participation.
The principles are the same, but the classification now places more emphasis on the individual's abilities rather than disabilities, and more emphasis is given to social context. In other words, it is a step towards the social model of disability and a step away from the medical model.

New classifications of the International Classification of Functioning and Disability:
Impairment - the loss or abnormality of a body structure or a physiological or psychological function.

Activity. The nature and extent of functioning at the person's level. Activities may be limited in nature, duration, and quality. Contextual factors (participation). Include the features, aspects, and attributes of objects, structures, human-made organizations, service provision, and agencies in the physical, social, and attitudinal environment in which people live and conduct their lives. Contextual factors include both environmental factors and personal factors

MEDICAL AND SOCIAL MODELS OF DISABILITY

Practitioners in the field of neurological rehabilitation need to be aware of these different constructs of disability. Neurological rehabilitation has come from an "illness" background. At least in the past, it has been generally carried out by physicians with the support of nurses and therapists and delivered to disabled people. This health and illness perspective of disability is known as the "medical" model. It assumes many things about the nature of the disability.

- Disability is individualized. It is regarded as a disease state that is located within an individual. Thus, the problem and solution may both be found within that individual.
- Disability is a disease state, a deviation from the norm, which inherently necessitates some form of treatment or cure.
- Being disabled, a person is regarded inherently as biologically or psychologically inferior to a non-disabled person.
- Disability is viewed as a personal tragedy. It assumes the presence of a victim.
- The objective normality state that professionals assume them a dominant decision-making role.

In general, the philosophy of medicine has been to treat and cure. However, in rehabilitation, these outcomes are unlikely, and in the early days of rehabilitation, the aim was to normalize as much as possible. Indeed this philosophy is reinforced by the initial definitions of impairment, disability, and handicap proposed by the WHO. Neurological rehabilitation is now moving away from a rigid interpretation of this model and moving towards the fundamental construct of disability that has been proposed for many years by disability lobby groups. That construct is termed the "social" model of disability.

The fundamental difference between these two models is that proponents of the social model suggest that the person's impairment is not the cause of activity restriction. However, rather it is the organization of society that discriminates against the disabled community. The proponents propose that if society would accept and accommodate disabled people, both physically and attitudinally, then disability as a concept would be made redundant. In the early years of the disability movement and rehabilitation practice, there was a general feeling of antagonism between health professionals on the one side and the disability movement.

In recent years individuals working in the field have tended to adopt a rather more helpful middle ground. Most disabled people clearly realize that health professionals have an important and central role in assisting disabled people in minimizing their activity restrictions. Obviously, this is particularly true in the post-acute setting— for example, after a stroke or traumatic brain injury. Even in longer-term disabilities, such as cerebral palsy or multiple sclerosis, health professionals still have a crucial role in preventing unnecessary complications and advising on appropriate interventions that reduce activity limitations and promote society's participation.

On the other hand, most health professionals realize that they cannot solve, nor should they try to solve, all the problems associated with disability. Many are a function of inappropriate attitudes and barriers in society. There is a realization that the health professional should act as a supporter and information giver rather than a doctor in treatment. The distinction between these two models is now rather blurred, and a more helpful attitude of a partnership between disabled people and rehabilitation professionals is now being achieved in many rehabilitation units and community teams

BASIC APPROACHES IN NEUROLOGICAL REHABILITATION

Rehabilitation is an active and dynamic process through which a disabled person is helped to acquire knowledge and skills in order to maximize their physical, psychological, and social functioning. This process can be conveniently broken down into three key areas:

- Approaches that reduce disability
- Approaches designed to acquire new skills and strategies, which will maximize activity
- Approaches that help to alter the environment, both physical and social, so that a given disability carries with it minimal consequent handicap

THE REHABILITATION PROCESS

There are a number of basic tasks associated with the rehabilitation process:

- To work in partnership with the disabled person and their family
- To give accurate information and advice about the nature of the disability, natural history, prognosis, etc.
- To listen to the needs and perceptions of the disabled person and their family
- To work with other professional colleagues in an interdisciplinary fashion
- To liaise as necessary with key careers and advocates
- To assist with the establishment of realistic rehabilitation goals, which are both appropriate to that person's disability and their family, social, and employment needs.

The last point encompasses another fundamental principle of neurological rehabilitation. **The process of rehabilitation is set around the establishment of goals.**

The first goal to be set is the long-term strategic aim.

For many, a long-term goal would be returning to a completely normal lifestyle. For others, it may simply be to return home and remain at home with careers' help. Once a realistic and achievable long-term goal has been established, the smaller steps needed to achieve that goal are determined.

If, for example, a long-term goal is to be independently mobile without aids, then achieving that goal can be broken down into a number of short-term sub-goals. This process may, for example, start with sitting without support, then standing without support, then walking with the assistance of one person, then walking with aids, and finally achieving independent walking. The goals must be precise. There is no point in setting vague and subjective goals as neither the rehabilitation team nor the disabled person will monitor where they are in the process. A useful mnemonic to remember what the goals should be is SMART:

- Specific
- Measurable
- Achievable
- Relevant
- Time limited

Realistic goal-setting implies that both the disabled person and the rehabilitation team need to know when the goals have been achieved. Thus, each goal is equally important to have a valid and reliable outcome measure attached to it. There is a chapter about an appropriate range of outcome measures later in this book. In summary, there are a number of measures that are designed to monitor overall disability and/or quality of life that can help assess progress towards the final long-term strategic aim.

Shorter-term sub-goals often need more specific outcome measures. Such specific measures need to be quick and straightforward. If improvement in mobility is being monitored, then a simple, fast, and reliable measure may be timed walking over 10 meters. It is important to remember that any outcome measure used must be specific, valid, and reliable otherwise, it is not worth using. It is also worth remembering that while an objective measurement is important, subjective opinion of the disabled person concerning progress towards the goals is equally important. The goal-setting process should never be rigid and will often need adjustment and re-evaluation as the individual progresses through rehabilitation.

THE REHABILITATION TEAM

It is important to emphasize that a key principle of neurological rehabilitation is the close working together of all relevant health professionals. Many neurological rehabilitation teams also need to involve other professionals outside the health service context, including those employed by social services or the employment sector. Many teams benefit from the input of a specialist lawyer. The essence of rehabilitation is that individuals go beyond simply working together but blur their roles and work together in an interdisciplinary fashion.

This would mean that the goals are set not discipline by discipline but according to the needs and requirements of the disabled individual. If, for example, a major goal is for an individual to climb stairs, then it is important that the correct techniques are not simply used in the physiotherapy sessions but are also used by nurses and other therapists throughout the rest of the day. A collection of individuals working within their discipline and setting their own goals does not count as a rehabilitation team.

PART 2

SOME CRITICALLY IMPORTANT STRUCTURES & CONDITIONS

Autonomic Nervous System

Surprisingly, so many people who face health problems and rehabilitation don't know about Autonomic Nervous System (ANS) and its vital importance for the body's normal functioning.

The autonomic nervous system is a component of the peripheral nervous system that regulates involuntary physiologic processes, including heart rate, blood pressure, respiration, digestion, and sexual arousal.

It contains three anatomically distinct divisions: sympathetic, parasympathetic, and enteric.

The primary function of the autonomic nervous system is homeostasis.

Apart from maintaining the body's internal environment, it is also involved in controlling and maintaining the following life processes:
- Digestion
- Metabolism
- Urination
- Defecation
- Blood pressure
- Sexual response
- Body temperature
- Heartbeat
- Breathing rate
- Fluid balance

The **sympathetic** nervous system (SNS) and the **parasympathetic** nervous system (PNS) - provide sensory input and motor output, respectively, to the central nervous system (CNS).

Sympathetic and parasympathetic divisions typically function in opposition to each other. This opposition is often viewed as complementary in nature rather than antagonistic. For an analogy, one may think of the sympathetic division as the accelerator and the parasympathetic division as the brake.

The **enteric** nervous system (ENS) is an extensive, web-like structure capable of function independently of the remainder of the nervous system and is chiefly responsible for regulating digestive processes. The ENS is composed of reflex pathways that control the digestive functions of muscle contraction/relaxation, secretion/absorption, and blood flow.

Sympathetic

Activation of the sympathetic (SNS) leads to overall elevated activity and attention: the "fight or flight" response. The SNS innervates nearly every living tissue in the body.

The sympathetic nervous system is responsible for regulating many homeostatic mechanisms. Fibers from the SNS innervate tissues in every organ system and provide physiological regulation over diverse body processes, including pupil diameter, gut motility (movement), and urinary output.

SNS functions include the following:
- Acceleration of heart and lung action.
- Paling or flushing, or alternating between both.
- Inhibition of stomach and upper-intestinal action to the point where digestion slows down or stops.
- General effect on the sphincters of the body.
- Constriction of blood vessels in many parts of the body.
- Liberation of nutrients (particularly fat and glucose) for muscular action.
- Dilation of blood vessels for muscles.
- Inhibition of the lacrimal gland (responsible for tear production) and salivation.
- Dilation of pupil (mydriasis).
- Relaxation of bladder.
- Inhibition of erection.

- Auditory exclusion (loss of hearing).
- Tunnel vision (loss of peripheral vision).
- Disinhibiting of spinal reflexes; and shaking.

Parasympathetic.

A helpful acronym to summarize the parasympathetic nervous system's functions is SLUDD (salivation, lacrimation, urination, digestion, and defecation).

Up to 80% of (parasympathetic) PNS fibers are sensory and innervate nearly all major organs.

PNS functions include the following:
- "Rest and digest" processes.
- Cardiac relaxation
- Promote salivation
- Expiration, contracting, and stiffening airways to prevent collapse.
- An ideal "early warning system" for foreign invaders and monitoring the body's recovery.
- Express receptors for interleukin-1, a key cytokine in the inflammatory immune response.

The PNS promotes the "rest and digest" processes;
The PNS innervates only the head, viscera and external genitalia, notably vacant in much of the musculoskeletal system and skin, making it significantly smaller than the SNS.

What is fascia?

Fascia: shell, sheet, or any other distributed cluster of the connective tissue formed under the skin to attach, apply, and separate muscles and other internal organs.

Fascial system: a network of interacting, interconnected, interdependent tissues, forming a complex whole, all cooperate for traffic.

Large fascial networks, including power transmission, sensing functions, and wound healing.
- fascial system consists of a three-dimensional continuum of soft, collagen-containing, loose and dense fibrous connecting tissues, which permeates the body. It includes fat tissue, advention, and neurovascular shell, aponeurosis, deep and

surface fascias, epineuria, joint capsules, links, membranes, tendons, visceral fascia, and all intramuscular connective tissues, including endo- / peri- / epimizy.
- fascial system interpenets and surround all organs, muscles, bones, and nerve fibers, giving the organism a functional structure and providing an environment that allows all body systems to work integrated.
- allows you to jump, react to load, and is able to regulate it
- the fascia is constantly renewing
- without fascia, muscles cannot function, keep its shape
- the number of receptors in the fascia is much higher than the number of receptors in the muscles
- fascia gives information about movement, condition, stress, pressure, and pain in the brain and autonomic nervous system

Functions of the fascia
1. Connection - one of the most essential features: supporting function / every blood vessel is surrounded by a fascial coating that connects with surrounding fabrics
2. Protection - protects against gravity and pressure, stress, injury, and invasion of objects (with skin) stabilizes and protects our bodies
3. Transportation - takes care of the transportation of lymph fluid
4. Power transfer and stability - fascia itself can, thanks to small contractive cells, build tension and maintain muscle strength. also, it transfers power to muscles. Continuum coatings, partitions, tunnels, and skin, takes care of the system of functional energy transfer.
5. Information system – fascia provides information about all movements, body posture, and coordinating effects in the brain.

What to expect after deleting fascias
- Can be loss power up to 40% in the muscle
- An inflammatory reaction
- Adhesions that lead to rigidity and restriction movement
- Immobilization. Microcalcination (fibrosis) when the wavy and elastic connecting tissue structure turns to calcinated, rigid, and vulnerable areas.

SPACTISITY
Spasticity is a muscle disorder characterized by tight or stiff muscles and an inability to control those muscles. Reflexes may persist for too long and may be too strong (hyperactive reflexes). The muscles remain contracted and resist being stretched, thus affecting movement, speech, and gait.

Spasticity usually is accompanied by paresis and other signs, such as increased stretch reflexes, which collectively are called upper motor neuron syndrome.

What Causes Spasticity? Spasticity is generally caused by damage or disruption to the brain and spinal cord area that are responsible for controlling muscle and stretch reflexes. In other words – due to an imbalance of signals from the central nervous system (brain and spinal cord) to the muscles, these disruptions cause muscles to lock in one place.

Spasticity can be a symptom of a variety of conditions and diseases, including:
- brain injury
- spinal cord injury
- stroke
- cerebral palsy
- multiple sclerosis (MS)
- amyotrophic lateral sclerosis (ALS, Lou Gehrig's disease)
- hereditary spastic paraplegias •   adrenoleukodystrophy (ALD)
- phenylketonuria
- Krabbe disease

Spasticity has several characteristics that differentiate it from rigidity:
1. Velocity dependence
2. Clasp Knife Phenomenon: Limb initially resists movement and then suddenly gives way
3. Distribution: Antigravity muscles being more affected
4. Stroking Effect: Stroking the surface of the antagonist's muscle may reduce tone in spasticity.

Diagnosis
The diagnosis of spasticity should involve a thorough medical history and physical examination, focusing on potential causes for the symptoms, to make the correct diagnosis and management recommendations. Essential factors to be considered include any traumatic events that may have affected the Central Nervous System (CNS), changes in medications, noxious stimuli, and intracranial pressure changes. Additionally, electromyography (EMG) can provide valuable information about the velocity of nerve conduction, magnetic resonance imaging (MRI) scans can help visualize causative damage in the central nervous system.

- The severity of the condition can be classified according to a clinical scale, such as the Ashworth Scale, Tardieu Scale, Physician's Rating Scale or the Spasm Scale.
- Management Interventions for spasticity may vary from conservative (therapy and splinting) to more aggressive (surgery); most often, a variety of treatments are used simultaneously or are employed interchangeably. Treatment options do not need to be used in a stepladder approach.

Neurorehabilitation comprises four main categories of spasticity management targets.

1. **Client care:** Preventing or treating contractures; preventing or treating pressure areas; proper positioning of the body on the bed/wheelchair; easy orthotics fitting.
2. **Movement improvement:** The unmasking of voluntary movements previously covered by significant spasticity in cases of incomplete lesions; accelerating the "spontaneous" recovery process; modifying the "immature" motor pattern; using new recovery techniques to promote guided neuroplasticity, e.g., robotic rehabilitation; new functional pattern in moving and walking.
3. **ADL's (Activities of Daily Living):** transfers, getting around, putting on clothes, personal hygiene, driving, etc.
4. **Quality of life:** Independent living; social and professional reintegration

Physiotherapy Spasticity is one of the components of the **Upper Motor Neuron (UMN) syndrome**. Still, it should not be considered in isolation when it comes to management strategies.

Management targets must function and is always patient-focused rather than aimed at reducing the degree of spasticity.

<u>**Current spasticity management options include the following:**</u>
- Therapeutic interventions (physical therapy, occupational therapy, hippotherapy, aquatics) and physical modalities (ultrasonography, electrical stimulation, biofeedback)
- Positioning/orthotics (including taping, dynamic and static splints, wheelchairs, and standers)
- Pharmacological If the spasticity is widespread, then systemic medication is used. Oral medications (such as baclofen, dantrolene, etc.)
- Injectable neurolytic medications (botulinum toxins and phenol)
- Intrathecal baclofen

- Surgical intervention (including selective dorsal rhizotomy and orthopedic procedures)
- Progressive Resistance Strength Training.
- Biofeedback combined with functional electrical stimulation and occupational therapy.
- Nabiximols (a specific Cannabis extract) effectiveness in MS-related spasticity combined with a PT program may improve the overall response to spasticity reduction.
- Shock wave therapy on flexor hypertonic muscles.
- Continuous ultrasound therapy over 5 weeks (frequency 1MHz and intensity 1,5 W/cm2).
- Cryotherapy, using cold packs (12°C) for 20-minutes.
- Electric Stimulation using agonist stimulation showed a significant improvement in Ashworth Scores, while antagonist stimulation increased stretch reflex-initiating angle.

If the spasticity is localized, then local medication (injection) is used:
- Botulinum Toxin (Botox)
- Baclofen (Inrathecally - High concentration more locally).
- Phenol / Nerve Block Surgical procedures are also indicated in some circumstances to correct the positioning of tendons or nerve pathways.
- Intrathecal baclofen therapy (ITB) may be used in severe cases, which involves direct administration of baclofen to the spinal cord, thus reducing the risk of systemic side effects.
- Orthopedic surgery or neurosurgery can also help remedy changes to the muscles, bones, connective tissue, or nervous system.

PARALYSIS
- Paralysis is the loss of the ability to move some or all of the body.

Types of Paralysis:
- Complete paralysis is when you can't move or control your paralyzed muscles at all. You also may not be able to feel anything in those muscles.
- Partial or incomplete paralysis is when you still have some feeling in, and possibly control over your paralyzed muscles. This is sometimes called paresis.
- Localized paralysis affects just one specific area, like the face, hands, feet, or vocal cords.

- Generalized paralysis is more widespread in your body and is grouped by how much your body is affected. The type usually depends on where your brain or spinal cord is injured.

Another classification includes:
- Monoplegia is a kind of generalized paralysis that affects just one limb.
- Diplegia affects both sides' same area, like both arms, both legs, or both sides of your face.
- Hemiplegia affects just one side of your body. It is usually caused by a stroke, which damages one side of the brain.
- Quadriplegia (or tetraplegia) is when all four limbs are paralyzed, sometimes along with specific organs.
- Paraplegia is paralysis from the waist down.
- Locked-in syndrome is the rarest and most severe form of paralysis, where a person loses control of all their muscles except the ones that control their eye movements.
- Paralysis can be spastic when muscles are tight and jerky.
- It can also be flaccid when muscles sag and eventually shrink.

Causes
- Paralysis is most often caused by **strokes**, usually from a blocked artery in the neck or brain.
- Some kinds of paralysis are caused by certain conditions or **diseases linked to specific genes**.
- Paralysis after a serious accident or injury – a severe **head injury or spinal cord (back) injury.**
- **Demyelinating diseases**. These happen when the protective coating around nerve cells, called the myelin sheath, is damaged over time. That makes it harder for neurons to send signals throughout the body. It weakens muscles and eventually causes paralysis. There are several demyelinating diseases, but the most common is multiple sclerosis.
- **Periodic paralysis.** This is caused by changes in specific genes. It involves random attacks of paralysis, often triggered by something in the person's diet.
- **Sleep paralysis**. This happens while waking up or falling asleep. Sometimes people who have sleep paralysis will also see things that aren't there (hallucinate).
- **Todd's paralysis.** This often happens for a brief period after a person with epilepsy has had a seizure, usually just on one side of their body.
- **Tick paralysis and Lyme disease**. Some ticks have neurotoxins in their spit glands that can cause paralysis, starting in your feet and legs and moving upward.

- **Muscular dystrophy (MD).** MD is when changes in genes in these proteins make muscles weak and cause them to break down over time.
- **HTLV-1 associated myelopathy.** Also called tropical spastic paraparesis (TSP), this type of spastic paralysis comes on gradually after infection with human T-cell leukemia virus type 1.
- **Motor neuron diseases (MNDs).** Motor neurons are the nerve cells that control the muscles you use to walk, breathe, speak, and move limbs.

There are two types of the Motor neuron: upper motor neurons, which send signals from the brain down to the spinal cord, and lower motor neurons, which get those signals and send them to muscles. MNDs are diseases that damage these cells over time.

- Upper motor neuron diseases, like primary lateral sclerosis (PLS), affect just the upper motor neurons. This makes muscles stiff and spastic.
- Like spinal muscular atrophy (SMA), lower motor neuron diseases affect only the lower motor neurons. This makes muscles floppy or flaccid, which makes them weak and sometimes causes them to twitch uncontrollably.
- The most common MND is amyotrophic lateral sclerosis (ALS or Lou Gehrig's disease), which affects both upper and lower neurons.

How is paralysis diagnosed?
- **X-ray:** This test uses small amounts of radiation to produce detailed images of the body's dense structures, such as the bones.
- **CT scan (Computed Tomography):** CT uses computers to combine many X-ray images into cross-sectional views of the body's inside.
- **MRI:** MRI uses a large magnet, radio waves, and a computer to create clear images of the body.
- **Myelography:** This test uses a contrast dye injected into the spinal canal to make the nerves show up very clearly on an X-ray, CT scan, or MRI.
- **Electromyography (EMG):** This test is used to measure the muscles and nerves' electrical activity.
- **Spinal tap:** A long needle is injected into the spine to collect spinal fluid.

PART 3
CLASSIFICATION

ICF

The International Classification of Functioning, Disability, and Health (ICF) is a framework for describing functioning and disability concerning a health condition.

The ICF is a classification of health, and health-related conditions for children and adults that was approved for use by the World Health Assembly in 2001, after extensive testing across the world involving people with disabilities and people from a range of relevant disciplines. A companion classification for children and youth (ICF-CY) was published in 2007. The ICF framework can be used in interprofessional collaborative practice and person-centered care. The ICF was approved by World Health Organization (WHO).

It provides a common language and framework for describing the level of function of a person within their unique environment instead of classifying the person by their having a specific condition. The World Confederation of Physical Therapy (WCPT) adopted a motion supporting the ICF›s implementation in physical therapy in 2003.

- Define standardized common unified and standard language and a descriptive framework permitting communication about health and health care across the world in various disciplines and sciences.
- Provide valuable tools to describe and compare the health of populations in an international context
- Helpful for diagnosis.

- The ICF instead provides a descriptive framework for health and health-related states.
- ICF is etiology neutral.
- Helpful for prevention and treatment.

The ICF classifies functioning and disability associated with health conditions.
- **Functioning** is an umbrella term encompassing all body functions, activities , and participation
- **Disability** serves as an umbrella term for impairments, activity limitations, or participation restrictions.

Relation ICD and ICF
- Two persons with the same disease (ICD) can have different levels of functioning (ICF)
- Two persons with the same level of functioning (ICF) do not necessarily have the same health condition (ICD).

ICF structure
- ICF defines components of health and some health-related components of well-being; the so-called domains
- Health domain
- Health-related domain, i.e., well-being (such as education and labor, and other environmental factors)
- Information is organized into two parts:

Part 1 deals with Functioning and Disability
a. Body Functions and Structures
b. Activities and Participation

Part 2 covers Contextual Factors
c. Environmental factors
d. Personal factors

Relation ICIDH and ICF
- The **International Classification of Impairments, Disabilities, and Handicaps** (ICIDH) is concerned with the consequences of diseases and provides a framework for managing chronic diseases.

- The ICF modernizes the ICIDH
- Terms with less negative connotations are used (e.g. activity instead of disability, Participation instead of a handicap).
- Definitions are updated
- More emphasis is given to social context

Underlying principles of ICF

Universality.
A classification of functioning and disability applies to all people irrespective of health condition and in all physical, social, and cultural contexts.

Parity and etiological neutrality.
In classifying functioning and disability, there is not an explicit or implicit distinction between different health conditions, whether 'mental' or 'physical'. In other words, disability is not differentiated by etiology. Shifting the focus from a health condition to functioning places all health conditions on an equal footing, allowing them to be compared using a common metric. Further, it clarifies that we cannot infer participation in everyday life from diagnosis alone.

Neutrality.
Domain definitions are worded in neutral language, wherever possible so that the classification can be used to record both the positive and negative aspects of functioning and disability.

Environmental Influence.
The ICF includes environmental factors in recognition of the important role of the environment in people's functioning. These factors range from physical factors (such as climate, terrain, or building design) to social factors (such as attitudes, institutions, and laws). Interaction with environmental factors is an essential aspect of the scientific understanding of 'functioning and disability.

So, ICF is a multi-dimensional concept relating to:
- ✓ Body functions - The physiological functions of body systems (including psychological functions).
- ✓ Body structures - Anatomical parts of the body such as organs, limbs and their components.

✓ Impairments - Problems in body function and structure such as significant deviation or loss.

✓ Activity - The execution of a task or action by an individual.

✓ Participation - Involvement in a life situation.

✓ Activity limitations - Difficulties an individual may have in executing activities.

✓ Participation restrictions - Problems an individual may experience in involvement in life situations.

✓ Environmental factors - The physical, social and attitudinal environment in which people live and conduct their lives.

Functioning and Disability include:

- **Body Functions and Structures**—describes actual anatomy and physiology/psychology of the human body.
- **Activity and Participation**—describes the person's functional status, including communication, mobility, interpersonal interactions, self-care, learning, applying knowledge, Involvement in a life situation etc.

Contextual Factors include:

- **Environmental Factors**—factors that are not within the person's control, such as family, work, government agencies, laws, and cultural beliefs.
- **Personal Factors**—include race, gender, age, educational level, coping styles, etc. Personal factors are not specifically coded in the ICF because of the wide variability among cultures. However, they are included in the framework because although they are independent of the health condition, they may influence how a person functions.

Key Points

- The ICD (International Classification of Diseases and Related Health Problems) classifies disease, the ICF looks at functioning. Therefore, the use of the two together would provide a more comprehensive picture of persons and populations' health.
- The ICF is not based on etiology or "consequence of disease," but as a health component. Thus, while functional status may be related to a health condition, knowing the health condition does not predict functional status.
- The World Health Organization defines "health" as "the complete physical, mental, and social functioning of a person and not merely the absence of disease." In this definition, functioning as classified in the ICF is an essential component of health.
- The ICF describes health and health-related domains using standard language.

Performance versus Capacity

- **Capacity:** what a person can do in a standardised environment e.g. during clinical assessment. It indicates the extent of activity limitation as a direct manifestation of a person's health status without assistance (assistance of another person, equipment or environmental modification).
- **Performance:** what a person actually does in his/her usual environment e.g. at home. It indicates the extent of participation restriction or the "lived experience" by describing all physical, social, and attitudinal environmental factors. It measures the difficulty a person experiences in doing things, assuming that they want to do them.

The gap between these two constructs reflects the impact that different environments can have on activities and participation. This gap can then guide intervention (e.g. on environmental factors) to help improve a patient's performance.

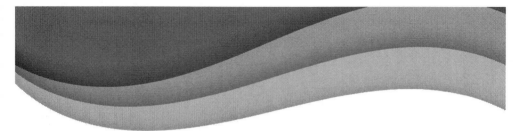

NEUROLOGICAL DISORDERS

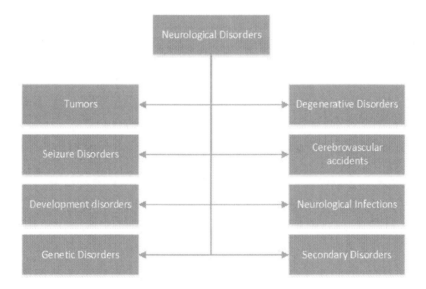

Neurological disorders are diseases of the central and peripheral nervous system, including the brain, spinal cord, peripheral nerves, cranial nerves, nerve roots, neuromuscular junction, autonomic nervous system, and muscles. Neurological diseases seem to be subtle in their clinical manifestations and are most prone to misinterpretations. They are becoming more prevalent, and the burden is increasing as the world's population ages.

Prevalence and incidence information of neurological diseases play an imperative role in assessing burden and treatment planning. However, epidemiological studies associated with the disorders face challenges, first, because the diagnostic criteria are prone to misclassification. Second, the diagnosis is based not only on clinical phenotype but also on sophisticated technologies such as magnetic resonance imaging or measuring biomarkers from cerebrospinal fluid (CSF) and serum that require specialist skills.

Third, the long variable gaps between the occurrence of disease and manifestation of symptoms get visible and observable among patients. In addition to it, in vivo pathological confirmations are very difficult. For this reason, there is a guideline that is being developed that consists of a checklist and recommendations known as "the standards of reporting of neurological disorders (STROND)" for the facilitation of improved reporting of prevalence studies of neurological diseases.

Mental and neurological illnesses together encompass disorders of the brain. According to the latest estimates, brain disorders account for 13% of global diseases exceeding cancer and cardiovascular diseases. Furthermore, according to the World Health Organization, mental illnesses burden the world more than any other chronic disease. Many epidemiological studies suggested that about one-third of the adult population suffers from mental disorders every year. More than 6 million people die due to stroke, and more than 50 million people have epilepsy, while 47.5 million people have dementia, and 7.7 million cases are reported every year. At the same time, globally prevalence of migraines accounts for more than 10% of Western countries' adult population.

Due to burden of disease, the 1990 **Global Burden of Disease (GBD)** study, a time-based metric was used to assess the disease that measures disability weighted by severity (years of healthy life lost because of disability or **Years Lost due to Disease [YLD])** and premature mortality or years of life lost (YLL). Both of them together are called **disability-adjusted life years (DALYs).** According to the GBD report, 13% of patients lived with **DALYs** due to neurological and psychiatric disorders, where only 33% of years lived with disability.

The WHO uses the terms **DALYs** to measure disease burden, and **YLDs** and **YLLs** tell about premature death due to disability. Neurological disorders such as epilepsy, Parkinson's disease (PD), dementia, migraines, cerebrovascular disease, and multiple sclerosis contribute to 92 million DALYs in 2005, projected to increase up to 103 million in the year 2030.

Classification Neurological disorders include epilepsy, neuro infections (bacterial and viral), brain tumors, cerebrovascular diseases, Alzheimer's disease and other dementias, migraine and other headache disorders, multiple sclerosis, and traumatic disorders due to head trauma. Many viral (i.e., enteroviruses, human immunodeficiency virus, West Nile Virus, and Zika), bacterial (i.e., Neisseria meningitidis and Mycobacterium tuberculosis), fungal (i.e., Aspergillus and Cryptococcus), and parasitic (i.e., Malaria and Chagas) infections can affect the nervous system.

Clinical manifestations and investigations.

The main causes of neurological disorders for different disorders, for instance, for multiple sclerosis it could be trauma, skull fracture, spinal cord injury, is caused by immunological factors, genetic disorders, stroke is caused by cerebrovascular accident, meningitis is caused by infection, neoplasia, diabetic neuropathy they are the metabolic disorders, environmental factors cause heavy metal encephalopathies. Chronic pain is frequent with many disorders. As the disease progresses:

1. altered sensation, i.e., hyperalgesia and allodynia,
2. altered emotion, i.e., reward deficit syndrome and depression anxiety,
3. altered cognition/integrative processing, i.e., memory,
4. altered pain modulation, i.e., increased sensitivity, diminishes the response to analgesics because of these symptoms.

Moreover, lifestyle factors such as tobacco use, less physical activity, obesity, alcohol, and specific diet such as Vitamin D have shown to develop MS, which all contribute to developing neurological diseases.

Specific tests for clinical neurological examination include mental status examination, which includes **Glasgow Coma Scale, cranial nerve examination, examination of the motor system, deep tendon reflexes, sensory system examination** includes provoking sensations of fine pain, touch, and temperature. Finally, **cerebellum testing** is examined by finger to nose test, assessment of gait, nystagmus, and intention tremor. At the same time, **neuroimaging (brain scans), angiography, biopsy, CSF analysis, computed tomography (CT) scans, discography, electroencephalography, electromyography, single-photon emission CT (SPECT), ultrasound imaging, and magnetic resonance imaging** also help in coordination with clinical tests to diagnose the disease.

Neurological disorders are screened by neurological screening examination, which is an essential procedure for neurological complaints assessment. It includes six areas:

1. **Mental status:** By assessing the normal orientation to place, time, space, and speech.
2. **Motor:** For checking drift, tone, and heel and toe walking.
3. **Sensory:** For cold and vibration.
4. **Reflexes:** To tap an instrument above a nerve to check a reflex which is emitted by nerve.
5. **Coordination:** By observing the patient's walk and finger to nose testing.
6. **Cranial nerves:** Checking the eyes by ophthalmoscope and assessment of facial muscle function and strength.

GENETIC DISORDERS

Genes are the building blocks of heredity. They are passed from parent to child. They hold DNA, the instructions for making proteins. Proteins do most of the work in cells. They move molecules from one place to another, build structures, break down toxins, and do many other maintenance jobs.

A genetic disease is any disease caused by an abnormality in the genetic makeup of an individual. The genetic abnormality can range from minuscule to major -- from a discrete mutation in a single base in the DNA of a single gene to a gross chromosomal abnormality involving the addition or subtraction of an entire chromosome or set of chromosomes. Some people inherit genetic disorders from the parents, while acquired changes or mutations in a preexisting gene or group of genes cause other genetic diseases. Genetic mutations can occur either randomly or due to some environmental exposure.

Types of genetic disorders:

- **Chromosomal disorders**
- The whole or part of a chromosome is missing or duplicated. These are large enough to be seen on a standard karyotype.
- Examples: Trisomy 21, Cri-du-chat, Turner, Kleinfelter
- Testing: karyotype

- **Microdeletion or microduplication**
- Part of a chromosome is missing or duplicated. These are often too small to be seen on a standard karyotype

- Examples: DiGeorge syndrome, Prader-Willi syndrome (deletion type), Smith-Magenis syndrome, Williams syndrome
- Testing: FISH – fluorescent in situ hybridization, aCHG – array comparative hybridization

- **Single gene disorders**
- A mutation on a single gene. Maybe autosomal dominant, autosomal recessive, X-linked.
- Examples: Cystic fibrosis, Duchenne muscular dystrophy, Marfan syndrome, Sickle cell anemia
- Testing: DNA sequencing, mutation analysis, deletion testing

- **Triplet repeat disorders**
- Exceeding the number of normal trinucleotide repeats in genes. The normal number varies depending on the gene.
- Examples: Fragile X, Huntington's disease
- Testing: DNA testing for number of repeats

- **Epigenetic disorders**
- The genetic sequence is not changed, but the expression of the DNA is altered
- Examples: Angleman, Beckwith-Wiedemann syndrome, Prader-Willi (methylation or isodisomy type)
- Testing: Methylation testing

- **Multifactorial disorders**
- Combination of genetics and environment
- Examples: isolated congenital heart defects, cleft lip, and palate, pyloric stenosis
- Testing: may be available if part of a syndrome, but usually no testing is available

- **Miscellaneous**
- Not otherwise categorized, and also includes:
- Associations or non-random association of anomalies without a known genetic basis, an example is CHARGE association
- Disruptions or morphological defect of a previously normal organ, for example, is amniotic bands
- Sequences of one malformation lead to other malformation; an example is a Pierre-Robin sequence

Traumatic brain injuries.

Traumatic brain injury is the leading cause of death and disability in children and young adults worldwide and is involved in nearly half of all trauma deaths. Many years of productive life are lost, and many people have to suffer years of disability after brain injury. Also, it engenders significant economic costs for individuals, families, and society. Many lives can be saved and years of disability spared through better prevention.

DEFINITION AND OUTCOME

If an external mechanical force hits the head, the brain will be displaced inside the skull. It can be injured against the solid meningeal membrane, the dura, or against the inside of the neurocranium. Acceleration and deceleration forces may disrupt the nervous tissue and blood vessels of the brain. All grades of injury can occur, ranging from no visible abnormality of the brain in cases of mild TBI to superficial bruising (contusion) and, in severe cases, dramatic swelling (edema) as well as large collections of blood (hematomas). Initial classification of TBI is based mainly upon the clinical examination which the physician carries out in the hospital's accident and emergency department.

DIAGNOSIS AND CLASSIFICATION

The diagnosis of (Traumatic Brain Injury) TBI can be evident in cases where a blow to the head is reported and when superficial wounds can be identified. But some patients are less clear-cut, and TBI may be present without any superficial signs of a head injury. Further classification of the brain injury is made to evaluate prognosis, identify patients at risk for deterioration, and choose appropriate observation and treatment.

The Glasgow Coma Scale (GCS) uses a points system to assess the best ocular, verbal, and motor responses. An average healthy person will obtain a **GCS** score (adding up the eye-opening score, the verbal score, and the motor score) of 15. Someone who opens his eyes only after painful stimulation, utters only incomprehensible sounds, and withdraws his hand only after pinching will be given a score of 8.

This scale permits the following classification of TBI after clinical examination: mild head injury (GCS 13–15), moderate head injury (GCS 9–12); severe head injury (GCS 3–8).

Disability Traumatic brain injury

is the leading cause of disability in people under 40 years of age. Disability can be classified in a simple fashion using the Glasgow Outcome Scale, Classification (GOS level), Description Dead Persistent vegetative state Awake but not aware Severely disabled Conscious but dependent

Mostly, patients with severe disabilities will have a combined mental and physical handicap. The rarest form of disability after TBI is the vegetative state. It may be transitory, subsiding after a month or so, but may persist in many cases. The persistently vegetative patient needs artificial nutrition and hydration and will have a markedly reduced life span, i.e., 2–5 years. In some cases, complicated ethical and legal discussions arise about the purpose of continuing life-sustaining treatment.

Disability after moderate or severe TBI may take various forms: Mental sequelae with personality change, memory disorders, reduced reasoning power, and apathy. A defective recent memory may be particularly incapacitating. They have disturbed motor function of the arm or leg. Speech disturbances. Epilepsy, which may develop years after the primary injury, is seen in 1–5% of patients.

REHABILITATION AFTER TRAUMATIC BRAIN INJURY

Although disability after mild TBI may have been underestimated, most patients will make a good recovery with the provision of appropriate information and without requiring additional specific interventions. Patients with moderate to severe TBI should be routinely followed up to assess their need for rehabilitation. There is strong evidence of benefit from formal interventions, particularly more intensive programs beginning when the patients are still in the acute ward. Neuropsychologists evaluate orientation, attention, intellect, memory, language, visual perception, judgment, personality, mood, and executive functions of patients with TBI.

Stroke

Stroke is one of the main non-communicable diseases of public health importance. After coronary heart disease and cancer, stroke is the most common cause of death in most industrialized countries. In general terms, stroke is a sudden neurological deficit owing to localized brain ischemia or hemorrhage. Most strokes are attributed to focal occlusion of the cerebral blood vessel (ischaemic stroke), and the remainder is the result of rupture of a blood vessel (hemorrhagic stroke).

WHO defines stroke as the clinical syndrome of rapid onset of focal (or global, as in subarachnoid haemorrhage) cerebral deficit, lasting more than 24 hours (unless interrupted by surgery or death), with no apparent cause other than a vascular one.

DIAGNOSIS AND CLASSIFICATION

Acute stroke is a medical emergency, and the clinician must diagnose stroke quickly and adequately. The diagnosis of stroke is made reasonably accurately on clinical grounds alone by specialists; however, in general medical and emergency-department settings up to 20% of patients with suspected stroke may be misdiagnosed, which indicates that infarction cannot be reliably distinguished from hemorrhage without brain imaging.

In diagnosing hemorrhagic stroke, computerized tomography (CT) is the most reliable method of demonstrating acute hemorrhage within the first week after stroke onset. Generally, a non-enhanced scan is all that is required. In the diagnosis of ischaemic stroke, CT may or may not show a definite infarct, but a normal scan does not necessarily mean that the patient has not had a stroke.

The proportion of visible infarcts also depends on the timing of scanning. Within the first few hours, few infarcts can be seen. It should be noted that less than 50% of infarcts never become visible on CT, especially in patients with milder strokes. In such cases, diffusion-weighted magnetic resonance imaging (MRI) would be a preferable method of investigation. In developing countries, patients may not give a clear clinical history, and neuroimaging techniques (CT and MRI) are not widely available, which frequently leads to imprecise diagnosis.

For classification and clinical differentiation of ischaemic stroke subtypes, **Oxfordshire Community Stroke Project classification** is frequently used. The ICH subtypes are mainly classified and characterized using topographical patterns, namely localization of intracerebral hematomas (clots) in the brain.

Rehabilitation.

Stroke survivors frequently suffer from neurological impairments, functional deficits, and handicaps. Stroke rehabilitation is the restoration of patients to their previous physical, mental and social capability.

Rehabilitation may affect each level of expression of stroke-related neurological dysfunction. It is of extreme importance to start rehabilitation as soon as possible after stroke onset. In stroke units, in severe stroke cases with a decreased level of consciousness, passive rehabilitation is begun, and active rehabilitation is initiated in patients with preserved consciousness. Several organizational models of stroke rehabilitation exist.

Rehabilitation is typically started in hospitals and followed by short-term rehabilitation in the same unit (comprehensive stroke units), rehabilitation clinics, or outpatient settings.

A multidisciplinary team approach and involvement and support, are key features also in the long term. Several studies have shown that different rehabilitation services improve outcomes, but less is known about the optimum intensity and duration of specific interventions.

The scientific basis for rehabilitation and neural repair has increased considerably. The reorganization of activation patterns in the brain after injury may be monitored by functional imaging studies (PET, functional MRI).

Neuroinfections

Infectious diseases that involve the nervous system affect millions of people around the world. Neuroinfections are of major importance since ancient times. Even with the advent of effective antibiotics and vaccines, they remain a significant challenge in many parts of the world, especially in developing nations.

Some of the more frequent neuro infections have a major impact on health systems. Infectious diseases that involve the nervous system are reported globally by 26.5% of WHO's the Member States and by 50% of countries.

Viral infections: HIV/AIDS, viral encephalitis, poliomyelitis, and rabies.

Mycobacterial and other bacterial diseases: tuberculosis, leprosy neuropathy, bacterial meningitis, and tetanus.

Parasitic infections: neurocysticercosis, cerebral malaria, toxoplasmosis, American trypanosomiasis (Chagas disease), African trypanosomiasis (sleeping sickness), schistosomiasis and hydatidosis.

Viral encephalitis

Acute viral encephalitis is often an unusual manifestation of common viral infections and most commonly affects children and young adults. Every day, more types of viruses are being associated with encephalitis. Its variable presence depends on the age group, geographical zone, season of the year, and the state of health of patients.

At a global level, it seems that the most common cause of epidemic encephalitis is Japanese B encephalitis, with 10–15 000 deaths per year, markedly more than for herpes simplex encephalitis. However, it must be considered that up to about 50% of viral encephalitis cases, no specific cause can be found, so the predominant type is challenging to determine.

Causes of viral encephalitis
- Herpes simplex virus (HSV-1, HSV-2)
- Other herpes viruses: varicella-zoster vírus, cytomegalovirus, Epstein–Barr vírus, human herpes vírus 6 (HHV6)
- Adenoviruses
- Influenza A
- Enteroviruses, poliovirus
- Measles, mumps, and rubella viruses
- Rabies
- Arboviruses:
    o Bunyoviruses
    o Reoviruses
    o Arenaviruses
    o Retrovirus
    o Papovavirus

Viruses enter the central nervous system (CNS) through two distinct routes: hematogenous dissemination or neuronal retrograde dissemination. Hematogenous spread is the most common path. Humans are usually incidental terminal hosts of many viral encephalitides.

Arbovirus encephalitides are zoonoses, with the virus surviving in infection cycles involving biting arthropods and various vertebrates, especially birds and rodents. The virus can be transmitted by an insect bite and then undergoes local replication in the skin.

Patients with viral encephalitis are marked by the acute onset of a febrile illness. They can experience meningeal irritation, focal neurological signs, seizures, alteration of consciousness, and behavioral and speech disturbances.

The diagnosis is made by immunological tests, neuroimaging techniques, electroencephalography, and, sometimes, brain biopsy.

No specific treatment is available for every encephalitis, and the illness often requires only medical support.

Parasitic diseases

Neurocysticercosis Cysticercosis is an infection by the larvae of the pork tapeworm Taenia solium. The adult tapeworm (flat, ribbon-like, approximately 2–4 m long) lives only in the small intestine of humans, who acquire it (taeniasis) by eating undercooked pork containing the viable larvae or cysticerci. A tapeworm carrier passes microscopic Taenia eggs with the feces, contaminating the close environment and contacts and causing cysticercosis to pigs and humans.

Human beings, therefore, acquire cysticercosis through fecal-oral contamination with T. solium eggs. Thus, vegetarians and other people who do not eat pork can acquire cysticercosis.

Recent epidemiological evidence suggests that the most common source of infective eggs is a symptom-free tapeworm carrier in the household. Cysticercosis should be seen as a disease mostly transmitted from person to person. In the CNS, the larvae or cysticerci can cause epilepsy, hydrocephalus, spinal cord involvement, stroke, etc.

Toxoplasmosis.

Toxoplasmosis is a disease caused by an obligate intracellular protozoal parasite termed Toxoplasma gondii. Human infection usually occurs via the oral or transplacental route.

Consumption of raw or undercooked meat containing viable tissue cysts (principally lamb and pork) and direct ingestion of infective oocysts in other foods (including vegetables contaminated by feline feces) are common sources of infection.

Transplacental infection may occur if the mother acquires an acute infection or if a latent infection is reactivated during immunosuppression. In immunocompetent women, a primary infection during early pregnancy may lead to fetal infection, with the fetus's death or severe postnatal manifestations. Later in pregnancy, maternal infection results in mild or subclinical fetal disease.

Most T. gondii infections are subclinical in adults, but a severe infection can occur in immunocompromised patients, such as those with AIDS and malignancies.

Affected organs include both the grey and white matter of the brain, retina, alveolar lining of the lungs, heart, and skeletal muscle.

Multiple sclerosis.

Multiple sclerosis affects around 2.5 million people worldwide: it is one of the most common neurological disorders and causes of disability of young adults. Although some people experience minor disability during their lifetime, up to 60% are no longer fully ambulatory 20 years after onset, with significant implications for their quality of life and the financial cost.

Multiple sclerosis (MS) is an inflammatory demyelinating condition of the central nervous system (CNS) that is generally considered autoimmune. In people with MS, the immune trigger is unknown, but the targets are myelinated CNS tracts. In regions of inflammation, breakdown of the blood-brain barrier occurs, and destruction of myelin ensues, with axonal damage, gliosis, and the formation of sclerotic plaques. Plaques (MS lesions) may form in the CNS white matter in any location (and grey matter); thus, clinical presentations may be diverse. Continuing lesion formation in MS often leads to physical disability and, not infrequently, to cognitive decline.

DIAGNOSIS AND CLASSIFICATION

As the above definition suggests, MS can lead to a wide variety of symptoms, affecting different parts of the body and with varying severity. Diagnosis of MS has always been clinically based, but many tests — notably magnetic resonance imaging (MRI) and more specific diagnostic criteria — are now available to assist the clinician. MRI, the examination of the cerebrospinal fluid (CSF), and visual evoked potentials help confirm MS's clinical suspicion.

In Asia, where the prevalence is reported to be low (1–5 per 100 000), the clinical presentation may be similar to that seen in Europe and North America, with manifestations suggesting cerebral, brainstem, cerebellar, optic nerve and spinal cord involvement (western type of MS) or may present with more restricted recurrent optic nerve and spinal cord involvement (opticospinal form or the Asian variant). The reason for this variation is not known.

To establish the MS diagnosis, a neurologist must demonstrate that involvement of the CNS is disseminated in time and space and exclude any other diagnostic possibility. Defined criteria are used to conclude whether the features fulfill the clinical diagnosis and allow for more precision, thus lessening the likelihood of an incorrect diagnosis.

Currently, the most widely accepted guidelines to the diagnosis of MS are the "McDonald Criteria." These criteria incorporate MRI to provide evidence of dissemination in time and space and enable the clinician to make an early diagnosis of MS. They also facilitate MS's diagnosis after a first attack (a clinically isolated syndrome) and in disease with insidious progression (the primary progressive form of MS), see below.

While these criteria have proved to be helpful in a typical adult Caucasian population of western European ethnic origin, their validity remains to be confirmed in other regions such as Asia, where some studies still use **Poser's criteria**. As the experience with MRI in MS builds up, it is expected that the McDonald criteria with minor modifications will become applicable worldwide. It is always essential that other conditions mimicking MS (such as vascular disorders, Sjogren's disease, and sarcoid) are excluded.

Rehabilitation.
Together with Rehabilitation in Multiple Sclerosis, **the European Multiple Sclerosis Platform (EMSP)** developed helpful guidance on this issue in their recommendations on MS rehabilitation services, one of the reference guidelines for their European Code of Good Practice in MS.

The essential components of successful neurorehabilitation include multidisciplinary expert assessment, goal-oriented programs, and evaluation of the impact on patient and goal achievement by using clinically appropriate, scientifically sound outcome measures incorporating the patient's perspective. While these principles are intuitively sound, the evidence underpinning multidisciplinary assessment and goal-orientated programs is weak.

Fundamental to the provision of robust evidence of the benefits of rehabilitation interventions is the use of scientifically sound outcome measures. In the field of MS, the limitations of **the Expanded Disability Status Scale** have been well aired, and it can be argued that the scale is even less relevant to neurorehabilitation as it fails to incorporate the views of the patient.

The issues relating to the management of symptoms that affect people with MS are identical to those concerning neurorehabilitation: the need for robust clinical trials based on scientifically sound outcome measures, multidisciplinary expertise, and patients' involvement. The frequency with which these symptoms affect people with

MS has been documented for various symptoms, including fatigue, spasticity, pain, and cognitive impairment. The need for a multidisciplinary and multimodal approach to symptom management is described in a recent review and is exemplified in the case of spasticity.

The delivery of care for people with long-term illnesses is becoming increasingly "patient-centered,» and culture of treatment by interdisciplinary teams is emerging. Within this model, the aim is to offer patients a seamless service, which typically involves bringing together various health professionals, including doctors, nurses, physiotherapists, occupational therapists, speech and language therapists, clinical psychologists, and social workers. Other professionals with expertise in treating neurologically disabled people cover dietetics, continence advisory and management services, pain management, chiropody, podiatry and ophthalmology services.

Epilepsy.

Epilepsy is a chronic neurological disorder affecting both sexes and all ages, with worldwide distribution. The term is also applied to a large group of conditions characterized by typical symptoms called "epileptic seizures", which may occur in the context of a brain insult that can be systemic, toxic, or metabolic.

These events (called provoked or acute symptomatic seizures) are presumed to be an acute manifestation of the insult. They may not recur when the underlying cause has been removed, or the acute phase has elapsed.

Epilepsy has been defined as "a disorder of the brain characterized by an enduring predisposition to generate epileptic seizures, and by the neurobiological, cognitive, psychological and social consequences of this condition.

The definition of epilepsy requires the occurrence of at least one epileptic seizure". An epileptic seizure is defined as "a transient occurrence of signs and/or symptoms due to abnormal excessive or synchronous neuronal activity in the brain".

These definitions recognize that a diagnosis of epilepsy implies the existence of a persistent epileptogenic abnormality that is present whether seizures occur or not, as well as that there may be consequences of this persistent abnormality other than the occurrence of seizures that can cause continuous disability between seizure occurrence (interictally).

Because it is often difficult to identify an enduring predisposition definitively to generate epileptic seizures, a common operational definition of epilepsy is the occurrence of two or more non-provoked epileptic seizures more than 24 hours apart.

Differential diagnosis of transient events that could represent epileptic seizures involves first determining that the events are epileptic, distinguishing between provoked epileptic seizures and a chronic epileptic condition.

Febrile seizures in infants and young children and ***withdrawal seizures in alcoholics*** are common examples of provoked seizures that do not require a diagnosis of epilepsy. If seizures are recurrent, it is next necessary to search for an underlying treatable cause. If such a cause cannot be found, or if it is treated and seizures persist, then treatment of seizures is guided by the diagnosis of the specific seizure type(s), and syndrome if present.

Types of epileptic seizure

I. Generalized onset
- Clonic and tonic seizures
- Absences
- Myoclonic seizure types
- Epileptic spasms
- Atonic seizures

II. Focal onset

o A Local
- Neocortical
- Limbic

o B With ipsilateral propagation

o C With the contralateral spread

o D Secondarily generalized

III. Neonatal

Because there are many types of seizures and epilepsy, there is no single course or outcome. Prognosis depends on the seizure type, the underlying cause, and the syndrome when this can be determined. Approximately one in 10 individuals will experience at least one epileptic seizure in their lifetime, but only one-third of these will go on to have epilepsy.

A number of idiopathic epilepsy syndromes are characterized by onset at a certain age and specific seizure types. Those that begin in infancy and childhood, such as benign familial neonatal seizures, benign childhood epilepsy with centrotemporal spikes, and childhood absence epilepsy, usually remit spontaneously. In contrast, those that begin in adolescence, the juvenile idiopathic epilepsies, are often lifelong.

Most of these are easily treated with antiepileptic drugs (AEDs), with no neurological or mental sequelae. Slowly, the genetic basis of these idiopathic epilepsies is being revealed, and there appears to be considerable diversity in that single-gene mutations can give rise to more than one syndrome, while single syndromes can be caused by more than one gene mutation.

The prognosis of symptomatic epilepsies depends on the nature of the underlying cause. Epilepsies attributable to diffuse brain damage, such as West syndrome and Lennox–Gastaut syndrome, are characterized by severely disabling medically refractory "generalized" seizures, mental retardation, and often other neurological deficits. Epilepsies resulting from smaller lesions may be associated with "focal" seizures that are more easily treated with drugs and can remit spontaneously as well.

When pharmacoresistant focal seizures are due to localized structural abnormalities in one hemisphere, such as hippocampal sclerosis in temporal lobe epilepsy, they can often be successfully treated by localized resection surgery. Some patients with more diffuse underlying structural lesions limited to one hemisphere can also be treated surgically with hemispherectomy or hemispherectomy.

Whereas 80–90% of patients with idiopathic epilepsies can expect to become seizure-free, and many will undergo spontaneous remission, the figure is much lower for patients with symptomatic epilepsy, and perhaps only 5–10% of patients with temporal lobe epilepsy and hippocampal sclerosis will have seizures that can be controlled by pharmacotherapy.

Of these patients, however, 60–80% can become free of disabling seizures with surgery. Advances in neuro diagnostics, particularly neuroimaging, greatly facilitate our ability to determine the underlying causes of seizures in patients with symptomatic epilepsies and design more effective treatments, including surgical interventions.

REHABILITATION.
The primary focus of care for patients with epilepsy is the prevention of further seizures, which may, after all, lead to additional morbidity or even mortality. The

goal of treatment should be the maintenance of a normal lifestyle, preferably free of seizures and with minimal side-effects of the medication.

Up to 70% of people with epilepsy could become seizure free with antiepileptic drugs treatment. In 25–30% of people with epilepsy the seizures cannot be controlled with drugs. Attention to the psychosocial, cognitive, educational and vocational aspects is an important part of comprehensive epilepsy care.

Epilepsy imposes an economic burden both on the affected individual and on society, e.g. the disorder commonly affects young people in the most productive years of their lives, often leading to avoidable unemployment.

Over the past years, it has become increasingly obvious that severe epilepsy-related difficulties can be seen in people who have become seizure-free as well as in those with difficult-to-treat epilepsies.

Pain associated with neurological disorders.

Pain can be a direct or an indirect consequence of a neurological disorder, with physical and psychological dimensions essential for its correct diagnosis and treatment.

Pain — Acute and chronic — is a significant public health problem that poses significant challenges to health professionals involved in its treatment. Chronic pain may persist long after initial tissue damage has healed: it becomes a specific health-care problem and a recognized disease in such cases. Adequate pain treatment is a human right, and any healthcare system has to provide it.

The current and most widely used definition of pain was published by the **International Association for the Study of Pain (IASP)**, which states that pain is "an unpleasant sensory and emotional experience associated with actual or potential tissue damage or, is described in terms of such damage." This definition was qualified by the Taxonomy Task Force of the association in 1994: "Pain is always subjective. Each individual learns the applications of the word through experiences relating to injuries in early life".

The physiological effect of pain is to warn of tissue damage and so to protect life. Pain is classified as nociceptive if it is caused by *nociceptors' activation (primary sensory neurons for pain).* Nociceptive pain can be somatic (pain originating from the skin or musculoskeletal system) or visceral (pain originating from visceral organs).

The sensory system itself can be damaged and become the source of continuous pain. This type of pain is classified as neuropathic. **Chronic neuropathic pain** has no physical protective role as it continues without obvious ongoing tissue damage. Pain without any recognizable tissue or nerve damage has its cause classified as idiopathic pain.

Any individual pain state may be a combination of different pains. A clinician's duty is to diagnose, treat and support pain patients, which means the identification of pain type(s) and their causative disease(s). It is also to provide adequate treatment aimed at the cause of the pain and symptomatic relief which should include psychosocial support. As the definition of pain reveals, pain has both a physical and a psychological element. The latter plays an important part in chronic pain disorders and their management.

TYPES OF PAIN ASSOCIATED WITH NEUROLOGICAL DISORDERS
Pain can be a direct or an indirect consequence of a neurological disorder. The former is seen in neurological conditions where there has been a lesion or disease of pathways that normally transmit information about painful stimuli either in the peripheral or in the central nervous system (CNS). These types of pain are termed **neuropathic pains**.

Pain can also be an indirect consequence of a nervous disease when it causes secondary activation of pain pathways. Examples of these types of pain include musculoskeletal pain in extrapyramidal diseases such as Parkinson's disease, or deformity of joints and limbs due to neuropathies or infections.

It is useful to distinguish between acute and chronic pain. Pain begins frequently as an acute experience but, for a variety of reasons — some physical and often some psychological — it becomes a long-term or chronic problem.

According to the IASP classification of chronic pain, this term refers to any pain *exceeding three months in duration*. Pain directly caused by diseases or abnormalities of the nervous system.

Neuropathic pain. In contrast to nociceptive pain which is the result of stimulation of primary sensory nerves for pain, neuropathic pain results when a lesion or disruption of function occurs in the nervous system.

Neuropathic pain is often associated with marked emotional changes, especially depression, and disability in activities of daily life. If the cause is located in the peripheral nervous system, it gives rise to peripheral neuropathic pain and if it is located in the CNS (brain or spinal cord) it gives rise to central neuropathic pain.

Peripheral neuropathic pain. Painful diabetic neuropathy and the neuralgia that develops after herpes zoster are the most frequently studied peripheral neuropathic pain conditions. Diabetic neuropathy has been estimated to afflict 45–75% of patients with diabetes mellitus. About 10% of these develop painful diabetic neuropathy, in particular when the function of small nerve fibres is impaired.

Pain is a normal symptom of acute herpes zoster, but disappears in most cases with the healing of the rash. In 9–14% of patients, pain persists chronically beyond the healing process (postherpetic neuralgia). Neuropathic pain may develop also after peripheral nerve trauma as in the condition of chemotherapy-induced neuropathy.

The frequencies of many types of peripheral neuropathic pain are not known in detail but vary considerably because of differences in the frequency of underlying diseases in different parts of the world.

Central post-stroke pain is the most frequently studied **central neuropathic pain** condition. It occurs in about 8% of patients who suffer an infarction of the brain. The incidence is higher for infarctions of the brainstem. Two thirds of patients with multiple sclerosis have chronic pain, half of which is central neuropathic pain.

Damage to tissues of the spinal cord and, at times, nerve roots, carries an even higher risk of leading to central neuropathic pain (**myelopathic pain**). The cause may lie within the cord and be intrinsic, or alternatively, be extrinsic outside the cord. Intrinsic causes include multiple sclerosis and acute transverse myelitis, both of which may result in paraplegia and pain

Spinal cord injuries result in pain in about two thirds of all patients. Other causes include **compressive lesions**, for example tumours and infections, especially tuberculosis and brucellosis. The former group comprises both primary CNS tumours and secondary tumours from breast, lung, prostate and other organs, together with lymphomas and leukaemias.

Pain indirectly caused by **diseases or abnormalities of the nervous system.** Pain arises as a result of several distinct abnormalities of the musculoskeletal system, secondary to neurological disorders.

43

These can be grouped into the following categories: musculoskeletal pain resulting from spasticity of muscles; musculoskeletal pain caused by muscle rigidity; joint deformities and other abnormalities secondary to altered musculoskeletal function and their effects on peripheral nerves.

Pain caused by spasticity. Pain caused by spasticity is characterized by phasic increases in muscle tone with an easy predisposition to contractures and disuse atrophy if unrelieved or improperly managed. In developed countries, the main causes of painful spasticity are strokes, demyelinating diseases such as multiple sclerosis, and spinal cord injuries. With an ageing population, especially in the industrialized countries, and rising numbers of road traffic accidents, an increase in these conditions, and therefore pain, is to be expected in the future. Strokes and spinal cord disease are also major causes of spasticity.

Pain caused by muscle rigidity. Pain can be one of the first manifestations of rigidity and is typically seen in Parkinson's disease, dystonia and tetanus. Apart from muscle pain in the early stages of Parkinson's disease, it may also occur after a long period of treatment and the use of high doses of L-Dopa causing painful dystonia and freezing episodes.

Poverty of movement and tremors may also contribute to the pain in this disorder.

Tetanus infection, common in developing countries, is characterized by intense and painful muscle spasms and the development of generalized muscle rigidity, which is extremely painful. During intense spasm, fractures of spinal vertebrae may occur, adding further pain.

Pain caused by joint deformities. A range of neurological disorders give rise to abnormal stresses on joints and, at times, cause deformity, subluxation or even dislocation. For example "frozen shoulder" or pericapsulitis occurs in 5–8% of stroke patients. Disuse results in the atrophy of muscles around joints and various abnormalities giving rise to pain, the source of which are the tissues lining the joint. In addition, deformities may result in damage to nerves in close proximity resulting in neuropathic pain of the "evoked" or spontaneous type.

Complex painful disorders. Complex regional pain syndrome (CRPS) refers to several painful disorders associated with damage to the nervous system including the autonomic nervous system. CRPS Type I was previously known as reflex sympathetic dystrophy, with the cause or preceding event being a minor injury or limb fracture. CRPS II, formerly known as causalgia, develops after injury to a major peripheral nerve. The symptoms exceed both in magnitude and duration those which might be expected clinically given the nature of the causative event. Also, patients often experience a significant reduction in motor function.

The pain is spontaneous in type with **allodynia and hyperalgesia.** Other features of the syndrome include local edema or swelling of tissues, abnormalities of regional blood flow, sweating (autonomic changes), and local trophic changes. Both conditions tend to become chronic. They are a cause of significant psychological and psychiatric disturbance, and treatment is a significant problem.

Management of pain of neurological origin.
The range of treatments available for pain directly caused by the nervous system's diseases includes pharmacological, physical, interventional (nerve blocks, etc.), and psychological therapies.

Neuropathic pain does not respond well to non-opioid analgesics such as paracetamol, acetylsalicylic acid and ibuprofen — a non-steroidal anti-inflammatory drug. Opioids have been shown to have some efficacy in neuropathic pain, but there are specific contraindications for their use.

Topical agents may give local relief with relatively little toxicity; they include lidocaine and, to a lesser extent, capsaicin cream, particularly in the treatment of post-herpetic neuralgia.

In selected cases, electrical stimulation techniques such as transcutaneous electrical stimulation or dorsal column stimulation may be used, but the latter in particular is expensive, which clearly limits its use.

Pain associated with spasticity and rigidity is treated with muscle relaxants. In the case of baclofen, it can be administered systemically or intrathecally. However, the latter route requires administration by a trained specialist and is unlikely to be freely available in developing countries.

Pain arising from joints secondarily damaged by the effects of neurological disorders is usually controlled using simple analgesics, for example paracetamol or a non-steroidal anti-inflammatory drug (NSAID).

Psychological techniques — and cognitive/behavior therapy in particular — are used to help patients cope with pain and maximize their social, family, and occupational activities. Research reveals that such treatments are effective in the reduction of chronic pain and absenteeism from work.

Physical therapy carried out by physiotherapists and nurses is an integral part of managing many patients with neurological diseases, painful or not, including strokes, multiple sclerosis, and Parkinson's disease, of naming but a few.

Relaxation techniques, hydrotherapy, and exercise help manage painful conditions that have a musculoskeletal component. There is good evidence that multimodal treatment and rehabilitation programs are effective in the treatment of chronic pain.

All health-care workers who treat pain, especially chronic pain, whatever its cause, can expect about 20% of patients to develop symptoms of a ***depressive disorder.*** Among patients attending pain clinics, 18% have moderate to severe depression when pain is chronic and persistent. It is known that depression is associated with an increased experience of pain, whatever its origin, and reduced pain tolerance. Therefore, the patient's quality of life is significantly reduced, and active treatment for depression is an important aspect of managing chronic pain disorder.

Cerebral palsy

Cerebral palsy (CP) is the most common chronic disability of childhood today. It is ubiquitous, and it occurs all around the world. Despite improved obstetrical and perinatal care, CP remains with us. As a result of injury to the brain, these children have motor defects that will affect them for their entire lifetime. Treatment often starts when they are infants and continues throughout their life, even into adulthood. The problems involved are complex; these children have mobility issues, but they can also have seizure disorders, gastrointestinal system problems, learning, perceptual difficulties, visual problems, hearing problems, and growth deficiency. Despite all these numerous difficulties, cerebral palsied children can be helped.

Cerebral Palsy (CP) is a disorder of movement and posture during infancy or early childhood. It is caused by nonprogressive damage to the brain before, during, or shortly after birth. CP is not a single disease but a name given to a wide variety of static neuromotor impairment syndromes occurring secondary to a developing brain lesion. The damage to the brain is permanent and cannot be cured, but the consequences can be minimized. Progressive musculoskeletal pathology occurs in most affected children. The lesion in the brain may occur during the prenatal, perinatal, or postnatal periods. Any nonprogressive central nervous system (CNS) injury arising during the first 2 years of life is considered CP. In addition to movement and balance disorders, patients might experience other manifestations of cerebral dysfunction.

Clinical findings Children with CP present with three types of motor problems. The primary impairments of muscle tone, balance, strength, and selectivity are directly related to the damage in the CNS. Secondary impairments of muscle contractures and deformities develop over time in response to the primary problems and musculoskeletal growth. Tertiary impairments are adaptive mechanisms and coping responses that the child grows to adapt to the primary and secondary problems. One typical example is gastrocnemius spasticity as a primary impairment leading to secondary ankle plantar flexion contracture and knee hyperextension in stance as an adaptive mechanism.

Clinical classification

Tonus	Lesion site
Spastic	Cortex
Dyskinetic	Basal ganglia - extrapyramidal system
Hypotonic / Ataxic	Cerebellum
Mixed	Diffuse

Anatomical classification

Location	Description
Hemiplegia	Upper and lower extremity on one side of the body
Diplegia	Four extremities, legs more affected than the arms
Quadriplegia	Four extremities plus the trunk, neck, and face
Triplegia	Both lower extremities and one upper extremity
Monoplegia	One extremity
Double hemiplegia	Four extremities, arms more affected than the legs

Associated Problems
- Intellectual impairment
- Epileptic seizures
- Abnormality of vision or oculomotor control
- Sensorineural hearing loss
- Dysarthria
- Oromotor dysfunction: difficulty sucking, swallowing, and chewing
- Gastrointestinal problems and nutrition

- Respiratory problems: aspiration leads to pneumonia in children who have difficulty swallowing. Premature babies have bronchopulmonary dysplasia. This leads to frequent upper respiratory tract infections. Respiratory muscle spasticity contributes to pulmonary problems.
- Bladder and bowel dysfunction: loss of coordination of bowel and bladder sphincters results in constipation and/or incontinence. Enuresis, frequency, urgency, urinary tract infections and incontinence.
- Psychosocial problems
- Gait Some children with CP cannot walk.

Spinal cord injury

Spinal cord injury occurs when something interferes with the function or structure of the cord. This can include consequences of a medical illness or trauma resulting in overstretching the nerves, a bump, the bone of the vertebra pressing against the cord, a shock wave, electrocution, tumors, infection, poison, lack of oxygen (ischemia), cutting or tearing of the nerves. Spinal cord injury can occur as a fetus develops from trauma or medical conditions.

Results of a spinal cord injury can appear differently depending on the type and location of the injury. The most common is loss of motor, sensory, and slowing of some of the body's internal organs (autonomic nerve function) below the injury level. In general, the higher in the spinal cord an injury occurs, the more function, sensation, and internal body functions will be affected.

Symptoms of spinal cord injury depend on the severity of the injury and its location on the spinal cord. Symptoms may include partial or complete loss of sensory function or motor control of arms, legs and/or body. The most severe spinal cord injury affects the systems that regulate bowel or bladder control, breathing, heart rate, and blood pressure. Most people with spinal cord injury experience chronic pain.

An injury in the spinal cord's cervical and thoracic area results in an **upper motor neuron lesion (UMN)**. This type of injury is associated with the development of tone (spasticity). Inside the body, organs are also affected by tone. Tone is easiest to notice internally by bowel and bladder function as small amounts of stool or urine automatically being expelled without emptying.

In the bowel's lumbar and sacral areas, a lower motor neuron lesion (LMN) occurs. This injury results in flaccidity. Very soon after injury, the muscles of the legs becoming smaller as the muscles lack tone. The bowel and bladder will fill but not expel stool or urine. Both can become over distended leading to major complications. Sometimes, the bowel and bladder will remove overflow waste without emptying.

Other Types of Spinal Cord Injury

Other less common types of spinal cord injury affect specific areas of the spinal cord. Anterior Cord Syndrome (sometimes called Ventral Cord Syndrome) is caused by lack of blood flow or lack of oxygen (infarction) to the front two-thirds but not the back of the spinal cord and in a part of the brain called the medulla oblongata. The result is loss of motor, pain, and temperature sensations, but where your body is in space (proprioception), and vibration sensations remain from the injury level down. Individuals with Anterior Cord Syndrome will note their body position by visually observing their environment instead of sense where their body is positioned.

Central Cord Syndrome is usually caused by a fall with overstretching (hyperextension) of the neck. Loss of function occurs from the neck to the nipple line, which includes the arms and hands. The torso has variable function and sensation. The lower body has an unaffected function but variable to total lack of sensation. Individuals with this type of injury usually retain the ability to walk but might have poor balance. Central Cord Syndrome occurs most often in elderly individuals due to decreased flexibility with age.

Posterior Cord Syndrome results in loss of light touch, vibration, and position sense starting at the injury level. The motor function remains. It is caused by trauma, compression of any length of the spinal cord's backside, tumors, and Multiple Sclerosis.

Brown-Séquard Syndrome is noted by one side of the body with motor function loss and the other side of the body with sensation loss. Depending on the location of the injury, the result can be presented as tetraplegia or paraplegia. Brown Sequard Syndrome can be caused by a tumor, injury, ischemia (loss of oxygen), puncture, infection, or Multiple Sclerosis (MS).

Cauda Equina is an injury to the nerve roots below L2, which results in leg weakness, bowel incontinence, urinary retention, and sexual dysfunction.

Conus Medullaris can be caused by an injury or disease affecting the nerve root's core of nerves. Damage to this area results in an incomplete spinal cord injury affecting leg function, bowel, bladder, and sexual function. Pain is typically present.

<u>Cord Concussion</u> results from a bump to the spinal cord. Much like a concussion to the brain, the spinal cord can be bruised or have message disruption for about 48 hours with the possible return of function thereafter. As with brain concussions, long-term dysfunction of various types can occur. Cord concussion is sometimes referred to as a 'stinger', especially in the sporting world.

Tethered Cord is an attachment of the spinal cord to the tissues in the tract where the spinal cord is housed in the body. This typically is an anatomical anomaly formed as a fetus and not detected until birth or later in early childhood. Sometimes, the tethered cord is not detected until adulthood. Surgery can release the cord if necessary. Tethered cord can appear after spinal cord injury due to complications of the injury.

Spina Bifida and other neural tube diseases occur in fetal development. The spinal cord does not form in the enclosed space of the vertebrae. In utero surgery (surgery before birth) can possibly correct spinal placement before a baby is born. Surgery after birth can correct the placement but with mixed results. Taking folic acid (vitamin B9) during pregnancy can reduce the risk of spina bifida. Inositol, a vitamin-like molecule, is being tested to assess if the prevention of neural tube defects is possible.

Diagnosing Spinal Cord Injury. Imaging using MRI or CT scans will provide information about a spinal cord injury, including the type and level of the trauma. This might not match up to your clinical exam, as the injury could be at one level. However, your level of function might indicate a higher level of damage due to swelling and other trauma or medical complications. In order to evaluate the functional outcomes of spinal cord injury, a physical examination is performed.

Spinal cord injury is evaluated using **the International Standards for Neurological Classification of SCI (ISNCSCI).** The same scale should be used to assess your spinal cord injury each time to be able to track your progress accurately.

Each level of the spinal cord is tested by assessing the dermatome or specific body section affected by the nerve at each level of the cord. In testing, the motor ability is assessed by moving every joint in your body. Assessments are made to see if you can move under your power, positioned, so gravity is reduced or unable to move. The sensation is assessed for gross and fine feeling. Both gross sensation, measured using a cotton swab, and fine motor sensation, measured using a sharp point, are tested. The sensation is measured by full feeling, feeling present but feels different and no feeling.

Using the **International Standards for Neurological Classification of SCI (ISNCSCI)** by a certified professional, the last fully functioning nerve becomes the level of injury. This might be the same on both sides of the body, but since there is a nerve exiting the side of each vertebrae, occasionally, there is some slight difference between sides of the body.

Levels of injury are assigned to indicate impairment. This is a method of communication for healthcare professionals to understand the extent of injury. The **ASIA Impairment Scale (AIS) from the American Spinal Injury Association** is available on the **International Standards for Neurological Classification of SCI (ISNCSCI)**. The AIS uses the following five categories (A-E):

A. Complete injury. This means no function or sensation is assessed at the end of the spinal cord.
B. Sensory incomplete. This level indicates sensory, but not motor function is retained, and no motor function is present within three levels of injury on either side.
C. Motor incomplete. Motor function is present at the end of the spinal cord.
D. Motor incomplete. Muscle function below the level of injury is against gravity.
E. Normal. No residual affects assessed.

A complete injury is often confused with a completely transected cord. The designation of complete injury means a complete interruption of messages through to the last nerve of the spinal cord. Rarely is the spinal cord completely severed. Complete severing might occur if a knife or bullet passes directly through the center of the spinal cord. There are typically nerve fibers that are still attached that may or may not be transmitting messages in complete spinal cord injury.

Secondary Conditions Due to Spinal Cord Injury

Besides a loss of sensation or motor function, injury to the spinal cord leads to other body changes. The body is still working below the level of damage. It is just that messages to and from the brain are not being communicated through the site of injury. The chart below indicates the secondary complications of spinal cord injury.

Body System	Secondary Complication	Paralysis Effects
Musculoskeletal	Calcium loss	Calcium loss from lack of movement through long bones of the legs, fractures
	Heterotrophic Ossification	Overgrowth of bone into soft tissue (muscle)
	Loss of muscle tissue	Replacement of muscle with fat, stomach pouch, scoliosis, skin breakdown
	Upper extremity pain	Shoulder pain from propelling a wheelchair, rotator cuff injury, bursitis, capsulitis
	Poor muscle tone	Scoliosis or curvature of the back
	Tone (spasticity)	Spasms of muscles of the extremities and inside the body in individuals with cervical and thoracic injuries. It can be painful or prevent correct positioning of the body.
	Flaccidity	Lack of muscle tone in the lower extremities and the body in lumbar and sacral injuries.
Nervous	The slowing rate of information processing	Complicated by injury to the brain
	Decreased balance and coordination	Spasticity
	Muscular pain and Neuropathic pain	The nerve pain from inefficient nerve transmissions
	Depression	Due to chronic illness/disability
Cardiovascular	Autonomic Dysreflexia	Misinterpretation of nerve impulses
	Orthostatic hypotension-low blood pressure, fainting	Poor return of blood through the veins
	• Deep Vein Thrombosis • Pulmonary Embolism	Pressure on blood vessels from external forces Poor circulation
	Edema	Poor return of fluid from the legs and arms
	Exercise intolerance	Ineffective distribution of oxygen in the blood
	Increased cardiac risk	Develops over time.
Respiratory	Decreased lung capacity	Restriction of breathing, poor posture
	Pneumonia	Infection in the lungs
	Mechanical Ventilation	In individuals with injury above C3

Gastric	Slower bowel absorption, Neurogenic bowel	Slowing bowel leading to constipation, enlarged colon, hemorrhoids, colorectal cancer
	Changes in ability to control cholesterol	Low HDL-good cholesterol
Urinary	Kidney stones	Less ability to filter urine
	Neurogenic Bladder	Failure to empty the bladder at the appropriate time
	Urinary Tract Infection	Bacteria in urine
Endocrine	Low testosterone	Reduction in hormones
	Higher incidence of Type II Diabetes	Decreased metabolism of insulin
	Sexual dysfunction	Erectile dysfunction in males, lubrication dysfunction in females
Immune	Slowing of the immune system reactions	Increased chance of infection
	Septicemia	A massive infection that affects key body organs.
Skin	Increase in skin breakdown or pressure injury	Decreased elasticity, pressure from bones, lack of movement
	Groin rash	From moisture in damp, closed areas.
	Nail care	Fragile nails or nail fungus
	Dry skin and calluses	Immobility
Digestive	Lower calorie needs	Obesity, the stomach pouch
	Feeling full all the time	Slowing moving bowel

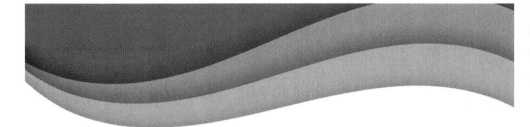

METHODS OF THERAPY

Standard Treatment
- Physical therapy uses treatments such as heat, massage, and exercise to stimulate nerves and muscles.
- Occupational therapy concentrates on ways to perform activities of daily living.
- Mobility aids include manual and electric wheelchairs and scooters.
- Supportive devices include braces, canes, and walkers.
- Assistive technology such as voice-activated computers, lighting systems, and telephones.
- Adaptive equipment such as special eating utensils and controls for driving a car.

Non-Standard Treatment

1. Treadmill or Locomotor Training
Locomotor Training is a rehabilitation approach that has been emerging over the last decade. It involves a kind of activity-triggered learning whereby practicing a series of specific movements (in this case, stepping) triggers the sensory information that somehow reminds the spinal cord how to initiate stepping.

Locomotor Training uses repetitive motion to teach the legs how to walk again. A paralyzed person is suspended in a harness above a treadmill, reducing the weight the legs will have to bear. As the treadmill begins to move, therapists manually move the person's legs in a walking pattern.

2. Functional electrical stimulation
Functional electrical stimulation (FES) applies small electrical pulses to paralyzed muscles to restore or improve their function.

FES is commonly used for exercise but also to assist with breathing, grasping, transferring, standing, and walking. It can also lead to improved bladder and bowel function. There's even evidence that FES may reduce the frequency of pressure sores and urinary tract infections.

- Bladder or bowel FES. Sacral stimulators are surgically implanted FES systems for on-demand control of the paralyzed bladder and bowel. The stimulator, called the Finetech-Brindley device, has a strong track record for improving bladder and bowel control in the vast majority of users.
- Upper extremity. The FreeHand system was well received, and people living with paralysis gained significant functions in grip, writing, eating, computer work, etc.
- Walking. There is an available device called Parastep that is FDA approved for some people with paraplegia (T4 to T12) to support stepping. Parastep, which Medicare has approved for reimbursement, facilitates stepping by firing leg muscles and uses a front-wheeled walker fitted with a control pad.

New technologies
- Brainwave communication: In clinical trials, people control computer cursors and open an email with just their thoughts. People can precisely move robotic arms using only brainwaves.
- BrainGate is an investigational brain implant system from a biotech company called Cyberkinetics that places a computer chip into the brain, which monitors brain activity and converts user intention into computer commands.

Overview of orthoses
Orthoses and braces are tools common in rehabilitation, though somewhat less than in years past. This is due in part to cost-cutting, limited clinical expertise, and reduced time in rehab. There is also a general feeling among many users that orthoses are cumbersome and appear too bionic or "disabled" looking.

An orthosis might be used to position a hand, arm, or leg, or magnify or enhance function. It can also be as simple as a splint or as complex as functional electrical stimulation (FES) brace for ambulation in people with paraplegia.

- **Wrist-hand orthosis.** Wrist-hand orthosis (WHO) transfers force from an active write to paralyzed fingers. This offers a grasping function for those with cervical injuries (generally between C4-C7). The WHO, also called a tenodesis splint, has been modified and simplified over the years, sometimes with batteries for power.

- **Ankle-foot orthosis.** An ankle-foot orthosis (AFO) is commonly used in people who have experienced strokes, multiple sclerosis, and incomplete spinal cord injury to assist the ankle and allow the foot to clear the ground during the swing phase of walking.
- **Knee-ankle-foot orthosis.** Knee-ankle-foot orthosis (KAFO) allows someone living with paralysis (usually L3 and above) to stabilize the knee and ankle. While it's very hard work, people using KAFO's, even those with no hip flexion, can take steps by swinging their legs while supported by forearm crutches.
- **Reciprocating gait orthosis.** Reciprocating gait orthosis (RGO) for children with spina bifida consists of a pair of KAFOs with solid ankles, locking the knee joints, legs, and thigh straps. Each brace's leg is attached to a pelvic unite with a hip joint, supporting hip flexion and extension. A steel cable assembly joins the two hip joints to limit step length.
- By rotating the torso, the user shifts the weight to the forward leg; this permits the opposite leg to move forward. This kind of walking is stable and balanced but slow and requires a great deal of energy.
- **Parastep.** A parastep is a "neuroprosthesis," a device that affects both the structure of the body (as a brace) and the nervous system (substitute for damaged nerves). It is a portable FES system that facilitates reciprocal walking by stimulating leg muscles on cue. The movement is a bit robotic but independent and functional for short periods of time.
- **Exoskeleton.** Exoskeletons and their role in both the rehabilitative care and home life of people living with paralysis became an important emerging technology only a few years ago. Essentially, exoskeletons are battery-powered bionic legs with small motors on the joints.
- **The Parker Indego is** a "powered lower limb orthosis enabling people with mobility impairments to walk and participate in over-ground gait training."
- **The Hybrid Assistive Limb (HAL),** developed by Japanese robot maker Cyberdyne, moves through the medical device approval processes.

CHIROPRACTIC

Basic Principles
The chiropractic profession is only a little more than a century old, but manipulation in its various forms has been used to treat human ailments since antiquity. Although no single origin is noted, manual procedures are evident in Thai artwork dating back 4000 years. Ancient Egyptian, Chinese, Japanese, and Tibetan records describe manual procedures to treat disease. Manipulation was also a part of the North and

South American Indian cultures. Certainly, Hippocrates (460–355 bc) used manual procedures in treating spinal deformity, and the noted physicians Galen (131–202 ad), Celsus, and Orbasius alluded to manipulation in their writings.

Both chiropractic and osteopathy chose to focus on the musculoskeletal system, although in philosophically divergent ways. A great emphasis on the somatic component of the disease, mainly involving the musculoskeletal system, and on the relationship of structure to function. Palmer postulated that subluxation, or improper juxtaposition of a vertebra, could interfere with the human nervous system's workings and with innate intelligence, that power within the body to heal itself. Both emphasized the role the musculoskeletal system played in health and disease.

The broad chiropractic model of health care is one of holism. In this model, health is viewed as a complex process in which all parts and systems of the body strive to maintain homeostatic balance against a dynamic environment of internal and external change.

The human body is perceived as being imbued at birth with an innate ability (innate intelligence) to respond to changes in its internal and external environment. Earlier health care pioneers saw this as proof of the healing power of nature, *vis medicatrix naturae*. This concept emphasizes the inherent recuperative powers of the body in the restoration and maintenance of health and the importance of active patient participation in treating and preventing disease.

Many different health care disciplines have described the presence of an inherent ability within the organism to influence health and disease broad-scope chiropractic care is committed to holistic health care and working with patients to optimize their health.

Although the chiropractic profession's major contribution to overall health is through the evaluation and treatment of NMS disorders, it is common for chiropractic physicians to counsel patients on other lifestyle issues such as diet, nutrition, exercise, and stress management.

The contemporary practice of chiropractic maintains its focus on the evaluation and conservative treatment of NMS disorders and the important relationship between the NMS system's functioning and overall well-being and health.

Dysfunction or disease of the musculoskeletal system in any form is viewed as having the potential to create disorders of the locomotor system that may lead to the individual's impaired functioning. This model is supported by the underlying principle that stresses the important interrelationship between the structure and function of the human body.

In addition to specializing in the adjustive (manipulative) treatment of disorders of the spinal and extremity joints, it is common for chiropractors to include other treatment procedures in patient management and health promotion. Common therapies applied include dietary modification, nutritional supplementation, physical therapies, and exercise.

The chiropractic profession considers the musculoskeletal system to be a clinically neglected component of the body. However, musculoskeletal disorders are common and account for significant amounts of lost time at work and recreation. Therefore, the musculoskeletal system deserves full consideration and evaluation whenever patients are seen, regardless of the complaint causing them to seek care.

The musculoskeletal system should be viewed as part of the whole body and subject to the same intensive diagnostic evaluation as any other body system. The musculoskeletal system is involved in so many alterations of function that it demands such attention and should not be removed from consideration in diagnosis, even when the initial problem appears removed from the musculoskeletal system. Moreover, the human musculoskeletal system accounts for more than half of the body's mass and is its most significant energy user.

The large amounts of energy required by the musculoskeletal system must be supplied through the other body systems. If the musculoskeletal system increases its activity, increased demand is placed on all the different body systems to meet the new, higher energy demands.

Chiropractic notes that the presence of disease or dysfunction within the musculoskeletal system may interfere with the musculoskeletal system's ability to act efficiently, which in turn requires greater work from the other systems within the body.

An important principle of chiropractic is that because the nervous system is highly developed in the human being and influences all other systems in the body, it plays a significant role in health and disease. Although the exact nature of the relationship between dysfunction of the musculoskeletal system and neurologic input changes to other body systems is not known, an enduring basic principle of chiropractic is that aberrations in structure or function can have an effect on health and the body's sense of well-being. The nervous system's impact on the body's ability to fight disease through the immune response demonstrate this concept.

The nervous system also communicates with the endocrine system to maintain a homeostasis state, defined simply as physiologic stability. The body's tendency to maintain a steady state or seek equilibrium despite external changes, referred to as *ponos* by Hippocrates, is the underlying theme in Palmer's original concept of innate intelligence influencing health.

Manual procedures and, specifically, the adjustment are applied to address local NMS disorders and to improve NMS function.

A consequence of improved NMS function may be the improvement in the body's ability to self-regulate, thereby allowing the body to seek homeostasis and improved health. In Haldeman's outline of this process, manipulative therapy improves the musculoskeletal system's function, which then causes a change in the input from the nervous system, which in turn may have a positive effect on other NMS tissue, organ dysfunction, tissue pathologic condition, or symptom complex. Reflex mechanisms that support these ideas have been documented, although the impact of manipulation on these reflexes has yet to be adequately assessed and demonstrated.

Manual therapy

Description
The International Federation of Orthopaedic Manipulative Physical Therapists defines manual therapy techniques as: "Skilled hand movements intended to produce any or all of the following effects: improve tissue extensibility; increase range of motion of the joint complex; mobilize or manipulate soft tissues and joints; induce relaxation; change muscle function; modulate pain; and reduce soft tissue swelling, inflammation or movement restriction."

According to the American Academy of Orthopaedic Manual Physical Therapists Description of Advanced Specialty Practice, orthopedic manual physical therapy is defined as any "hands-on" treatment provided by the physical therapist.

Treatment may include moving joints in specific directions and at different speeds to regain movement (joint mobilization and manipulation), muscle stretching, passive movements of the affected body part, or having the patient move the body part against the therapist's resistance to improve muscle activation and timing. Selected specific soft tissue techniques may also be used to improve the mobility and function of tissue and muscles."

Three Paradigms for Manual Therapy Therapeutic Effects
1. **Physiological**: positive placebo response
2. **Biomechanical and Physical:** facilitates repair and tissue modeling
3. **Psychological**: pain relief via- stimulates gating mechanism; muscle inhibition; reduction of nociceptive activity; reduced intraarticular or periarticular pressure

Techniques Include
- Traction
- Massage
- Trigger point therapy
- Active release technique
- Assisted Active Range of motion
- Passive Range of motion
- Lymph drainage
- Stretches
- Instrumental assisted soft tissue mobilization
- Joint Manipulation
- Joint Mobilisation
- Trans-anal/trans-vaginal massage/manipulations
- Intraoral manipulations

Bordering techniques (Manual therapy can include)
- Chiropractic
- Kinesiotherapy
- Massage
- Myofascial release
- Osteopathy
- Tendon-ligament gymnastics
- Stretching

Guide to Grading of Mobilisations/Manipulations

Maitland Joint Mobilization Grading Scale:
Grade I - Small amplitude rhythmic oscillating mobilization in the early range of movement
Grade II - Large amplitude rhythmic oscillating mobilization in the midrange of movement
Grade III - Large amplitude rhythmic oscillating mobilization to the point of limitation in range of movement
Grade IV - Small amplitude rhythmic oscillating mobilization at the end of the available range of movement
Grade V (Thrust Manipulation) - Small amplitude, quick thrust at the end of the possible range of movement

Kaltenborn Traction Grading Scale:
Grade I - Neutralises joint pressure without separation of joint surfaces
Grade II - Separates articulating surfaces, taking up the slack or eliminating play within the joint capsule
Grade III - Stretching of soft tissue surrounding joint

Contraindications to Manual Therapy.
- Neurological disease-causing potential cord compression Eg. Syringomyelia
- Myelopathy (eg. acute spinal injury, Myelitis)
- Cauda equina syndrome
- Osteoporosis
- Some surgical interventions
- Psycho-emotional excited state
- Marked hypermobility and severe Instability
- Spinal Stenosis
- Local malignancy
- Local infection
- Fracture
- Vertebral artery vascular compromise
- Inflammatory Processes
- Destructive Processes Eg. tumor or metastatic spread

If elicited through history, further workup is necessary. It should include the appropriate laboratory tests, radiographs, as well as CT scans and bone scans, MRI, etc., depending on the individual clinical situation.

Massage

Description
Massage therapy is the scientific manipulation of the body's soft tissues to normalize those tissues and consists of a group of manual techniques that include applying fixed or movable pressure, holding, and/or causing movement to parts of the body. While massage therapy is applied primarily with the hands, sometimes the forearms or elbows are used. These techniques affect the muscular, skeletal, circulatory, lymphatic, nervous, and other body systems.

Purpose
Generally, massage is delivered to improve blood and lymph flow (fluid in lymph glands, part of the immune system), reduce muscular tension or flaccidity, affect the nervous system through stimulation or sedation, and enhance tissue healing. Therapeutic massage may be recommended for children and adults to deliver benefits such as the following:

- reducing muscle tension and stiffness
- relieving muscle spasms
- increasing joint and limb flexibility and range of motion
- increasing ease and efficiency of movement
- relieving points of tension and overall stress; inducing relaxation
- promoting deeper and easier breathing
- improving blood circulation and movement of lymph
- relieving tension-related headaches and eyestrain
- promoting faster healing of soft tissue injuries, such as pulled muscles and sprained ligaments
- reducing pain and swelling related to injuries
- reducing the formation of scar tissue following soft tissue injuries
- enhancing health and nourishment of skin
- improving posture by changing tension patterns that affect posture
- reducing emotional or physical stress and reducing anxiety
- promoting feelings of well-being
- increasing awareness of the mind-body connection and improving mental awareness and alertness generally

Techniques Include
- Effleurage (Stroking)
- Petrissage (Kneading)
  o squeezing
  o Picking up
  o Shaking
  o Rolling
  o Wringing
- Percussion/Tapotement Manipulations
  o Hacking
  o Clapping
  o Beating
  o Pounding
  o Vibrations
- Myofascial Release
- Trigger points therapy
- Deep Transverse Frictions
- Compression massage
- Cross-Fibre massage

Contraindications to Massage treatment
Total Contraindications
- Fever
- Contagious diseases, including any cold or flu, no matter how mild it may seem
- Under the influence of drugs or alcohol-including prescription pain medication
- Recent operations or acute injuries
- Neuritis
- Skin diseases

Local Contraindications
- Varicose veins
- Undiagnosed lumps or bumps
- Pregnancy
- Bruising
- Cuts
- Abrasions
- Sunburn
- Undiagnosed pain
- Inflammation, including arthritis

Medical Contraindications

- Cardio-vascular conditions (thrombosis, phlebitis, hypertension, heart conditions)
- Any condition already being treated by a medical practitioner
- Edema
- Psoriasis or eczema
- High blood pressure
- Osteoporosis
- Cancer
- Nervous or psychotic conditions
- Heart problems, angina, those with pacemakers
- Epilepsy
- Diabetes
- Bell's palsy, trapped or pinched nerves
- Gynecological infections

LASER THERAPY

Laser therapy uses monochromatic light emission from high intensity super luminous diodes when the light source is placed in contact with the skin allowing the photon energy to penetrate the soft tissue, where it interacts with Various intracellular biomolecules resulting in the restoration of normal cell functions and enhancement of the body's healing processes.

Laser therapy is low-intensity laser therapy that stimulates healing while using low levels of light.

The technique is called "cold" laser therapy because the low levels of light aren't enough to heat the body's tissue. The level of light is low when compared to other forms of laser therapy, such as those used to destroy tumors and coagulate tissue.

Cold laser therapy is also known as:
- low-level laser therapy (LLLT)
- low-power laser therapy (LPLT)
- soft laser biostimulation
- photobiomodulation

How Does Laser Therapy Work?

When a cell is working to repair itself, it needs a great deal of energy. Most cells continue to work at their usual rate, which is why the repair of some tissues takes so long. In some instances, the cells stay so busy dealing with inflammation and bi-products that are present in the injured tissue; they don't have enough energy left to provide effective repair. With the use of lasers, the cells are stimulated, and their activity is increased to perform better, faster, and more effectively. The result is enhanced wound and injury healing in a shorter period of time.

The light from the laser stimulates the cell's mitochondria into hyperactivity. The Krebs Cycle of metabolism occurs on this structure's inner membrane, liberating energy from the chemical bonds present in ATP (adenosine triphosphate) molecules. The cell is provided with more energy and is now in an optimum condition to play its part in the healing process.

The following list of physiological & cellular level effects is compiled from several reviews & research papers. It does not claim to be complete or guaranteed for the in vivo situation. It does however, illustrate the range & scope of photobioactivation effects.

- Altered cell proliferation
- Altered cell motility
- Activation of phagocytes
- Stimulation of immune responses
- Increased cellular metabolism
- Stimulation of macrophages
- Stimulation of mast cell degranulation
- Activation & proliferation of fibroblasts
- Alteration of cell membrane potentials
- Stimulation of angiogenesis
- Alteration of action potentials
- Altered prostaglandin production
- Altered endogenous opioid production

What Conditions/Injuries can be treated by Laser Therapy?
- acne and acne scars
- Alzheimer's disease
- arthritis
- bursitis
- calcifications
- carpal tunnel syndrome
- chondromalacia patella

- degenerative disc disease
- dermatitis and rashes
- edema, or swelling of the skin
- fibromyalgia
- fractures with soft tissue damage
- ligament and tendon tears
- ligament sprains
- lower back pain
- muscle strains
- neck pain
- pain associated with muscle spasms
- Parkinson's disease
- plantar fasciitis
- psoriasis
- rheumatoid arthritis (RA)
- rotator cuff tears
- skin rejuvenation
- spinal cord injury
- sprains and strains
- tendonitis
- tennis and golfer's elbow
- tennis elbow
- TMJ
- vitiligo
- whiplash
- wounds

Extracorporeal SHOCK WAVE THERAPY

Shockwave therapy is a non-invasive treatment that creates a series of low-energy acoustic wave pulsations directly applied to an injury through a person's skin via a gel medium.

Mechanism of Action
- Pain reduction: the intensive pulses transmitted from the handpiece to the tissue help inhibit the transmission of the pain signal (Gate Control theory)
- Increased metabolism: shock waves influence the tissue on a cellular level, promoting the release of pain inhibiting and inflammatory inhibiting substances

- Revascularisation: repeated shock waves influence the blood flow, promoting tissue healing and regeneration
- Reduced muscle tone: shock waves help restore a normalized muscular tone by reducing the impact of pain on muscle tone.

In other words, EWWT promotes neovascularization at the tendon-bone junction, stimulates proliferation of tenocytes and osteoprogenitor differentiation, increases leukocyte infiltration, and amplifies growth factor and protein synthesis to stimulate collagen synthesis and tissue remodeling.

INDICATIONS
Shock Waves as a Treatment Modality for Spasticity Reduction and Recovery Improvement in Post-Stroke Adults, cerebral palsy, epicondylitis, and multiple sclerosis.

Widely used in the following conditions:
- Achilles tendonitis
- Back pain
- Bursitis
- Calcifications
- Chronic Tendinopathy
- Heel spurs
- Hip Pain
- Iliotibial band friction syndrome
- Jumper's Knee
- Medial Tibial Stress Syndrome
- Painful Shoulder
- Patellar tendonitis
- Plantar fasciitis
- Shin splints
- Tennis and golfers elbow

ULTRASOUND THERAPY
Ultrasound is a form of mechanical energy (not electrical). The normal human sound range is from 16 Hz to 15-20,000 Hz. Beyond this upper limit, the mechanical vibration is known as ultrasound.

The therapeutic effects of Ultrasound are generally divided into THERMAL & NON-THERMAL.

Thermal

Ultrasound can be used to selectively raise the temperature of particular tissues due to its mode of action. Among the more effectively heated tissues are the periosteum, collagenous tissues (ligament, tendon & fascia) & fibrotic muscle.

If the temperature of the damaged tissues is raised to 40 45°C, then a hyperemia will result, the effect of which will be therapeutic.

Also, temperatures in this range are also thought to help initiate the resolution of chronic inflammatory states.

Non-Thermal

The nonthermal effects of Ultrasound are attributed primarily to a combination of CAVITATION and ACOUSTIC STREAMING. There appears to be little by way of convincing evidence to support the notion of MICROMASSAGE though it does sound rather appealing.

CAVITATION - relates to the formation of gas-filled voids within the tissues & body fluids. There are 2 types of cavitation, STABLE & UNSTABLE which have very different effects.

STABLE CAVITATION does seem to occur at therapeutic doses of Ultrasound. This is the formation & growth of gas bubbles by the accumulation of dissolved gas in the medium. They take 1000 cycles to reach their maximum size. The `cavity' acts to enhance the acoustic streaming phenomena (see below) &, as such, would appear to be beneficial.

UNSTABLE (TRANSIENT) CAVITATION is forming bubbles at the low-pressure part of the Ultrasound cycle. These bubbles then collapse very quickly, releasing a large amount of energy detrimental to tissue viability. There is no evidence suggesting that this phenomenon occurs at therapeutic levels if a good technique is used.

ACOUSTIC STREAMING is described as a small-scale eddying of fluids near a vibrating structure such as cell membranes & the surface of a stable cavitation gas bubble. This phenomenon is known to affect diffusion rates & membrane permeability. Sodium-ion permeability is altered, resulting in changes in the cell membrane potential. Calcium ion transport is modified, which leads to an alteration in the enzyme control mechanisms of various metabolic processes, especially concerning protein synthesis & cellular secretions.

The result of the combined effects of stable cavitation and acoustic streaming is that the cell membrane becomes 'excited' (up-regulates), thus increasing the whole cell's activity levels. The Ultrasound energy acts as a trigger for this process, but it is the increased cellular activity that is in effect responsible for the therapeutic benefits of the modality.

MICROMASSAGE is a mechanical effect that appears to have been attributed less importance. In essence, the sound wave traveling through the medium is claimed to cause molecules to vibrate, possibly enhancing tissue fluid interchange & affecting tissue mobility.

1. Ultrasound and Tissue Repair

The process of tissue repair is a complex series of cascaded, chemically mediated events that lead to scar tissue production that constitutes an effective material to restore the continuity of the damaged tissue.

2. Ultrasound and Inflammation

During the inflammatory phase, Ultrasound has a stimulating effect on the mast cells, platelets, white cells with phagocytic roles, and macrophages.

Application of ultrasound induces mast cells' degranulation, causing the release of arachidonic acid, which is a precursor for the synthesis of prostaglandins and leukotriene – which act as inflammatory mediators.

By increasing the activity of these cells, the overall influence of therapeutic

The inflammatory response is essential to the effective repair of tissue. The more efficiently the process can complete, the more effectively the tissue can progress to the next phase (proliferation).

3. Ultrasound and Proliferation

During the proliferative phase (scar production) Ultrasound has a stimulative effect (cellular up-regulation), though the primary active targets are now the fibroblasts, endothelial cells, and myofibroblasts.

Ultrasound is pro-proliferative in the same way that it is pro-inflammatory – it does not change the normal proliferative phase but maximizes its efficiency – optimally producing the required scar tissue.

4. Ultrasound and Remodelling

During the remodeling phase of repair, the somewhat generic scar produced in the initial stages is refined. It adopts functional characteristics of the tissue that it is repairing. A scar in the ligament will not 'become' ligament but will behave more like a ligamentous tissue.

A number of processes achieve this, but mainly related to the collagen fibers' orientation in the developing scar and the change in collagen type, from predominantly Type III collagen to a

The application of therapeutic ultrasound can influence the remodeling of the scar tissue in that it appears to be capable of enhancing the appropriate orientation of the newly formed collagen fibers and also to the collagen profile change from mainly Type III to a more dominant Type I construction, thus increasing tensile strength and enhancing scar mobility.

Indications for Ultrasound
- bursitis
- capsulitis
- chronic or subacute inflammation of the joints and nerves
- chronic pain syndromes and contractures (limitation of passive movements)
- degenerative joint diseases
- digestion (peptic ulcer and duodenal ulcer, biliary dyskinesia)
- epicondylitis
- genitourinary system (salpingo-oophoritis, adnexitis, cervical erosion, prostatitis)
- hydroadenitis
- inflammatory and degenerative-dystrophic diseases of the joints with severe pain syndrome (arthritis, arthrosis, rheumatoid arthritis, osteochondrosis, periarthritis, epicondylitis)
- inflammatory diseases of peripheral nerves (neuritis and neuralgia, radiculitis)
- keloid scars
- ligament sprains
- mastitis
- muscle strain
- postoperative and post-injection infiltrates

VISCERAL MANIPULATION

It's one of my favorite themes due to the unique effects of the whole organism. Deep links between gut and brain, gut and Autonomous Nervous System, gut and metabolism, gut and pain, gut and joints, gut and respiration, gut and stroma. Visceral manipulation involves abdominal massage that combines various movements to strip away the adhesions. The goal is to restore the pliable, mobile state that helps organs get the circulation, nutrients, and suppleness they need to function correctly.

I have traveled around the world a lot, gaining knowledge of traditional and conventional medicine used in different cultures. And in ALL Cultures of traditional medicine, in India, China, Vietnam, Thailand, Indonesia, Ecuador, South Korea, Russia, Pakistan, etc., you will find this "mystical" technique. Current knowledge of the Microbiome and Microbiota's role in human life supports the importance of the Visceral Manipulation and understanding that after the brain, the second body part, contained a pool of neurons, is the gut.

Visceral manipulation is used to locate and solve problems throughout the body. It encourages your natural mechanisms to improve your organs' functioning, dissipate the negative effects of stress, enhance the musculoskeletal system's mobility through the connective tissue attachments, and general influence metabolism.

Visceral massage, as performed, serve as a useful form of vagal stimulation. "The vagus nerve may play an important role in pain modulation by inhibiting inflammation, oxidative stress, and sympathetic activity, and possibly by inducing a brain activation pattern that may be incongruent with the brain matrix of pain. Finally, vagal activation may mediate or work in synergism with the effects of the opioid system in pain modulation.

All these mechanisms are thought to influence neuronal hyperexcitability, culminating in the perception of less pain. For all the above neurobiological reasons, it justified increasing vagal nerve activity to reduce pain as this targets all five mechanisms with one intervention. The vagus nerve has been attributed experimentally to influence pain in various ways; deep breathing will augment vagal activity and has been shown to reduce pain. In all cases, it appears that vagal stimulation influences central pain processing rather than peripheral nociceptor activity.

There are also clear links between this research and study by neuroanatomist A.D (Bud) Craig, who provides clinical evidence regarding the relationship between viscera and the brain's area called the insular cortex. Craig spent nine years studying the neural pathways from the viscera to the anterior insular cortex. He claims that insular function will enable deep insights into the neural basis for subjectivity, feelings, volition, individual personality, belief, and self-modulation.

Visceral massage is a metaphysical experience paralleled by biological responses. There is a running dialogue between the gut and the brain that an experienced massage therapist can facilitate by providing a positive connection between them. While we have addressed some of the science and ancient art connected with visceral massage therapy, there are many more components to understanding how therapeutic massage techniques can address the sensitive digestive system and the emotions related to the brain-gut connection. Visceral massage is part of both functional medicine and ancient traditional therapy. It is an emerging therapeutic area for us in clinical practice, addressing conditions such as IBS, lower back pain, and a range of both gut issues and emotional concerns.

Indications:
- Acute Disorders: Whiplash Seatbelt Injuries Chest or Abdominal Sports Injuries Concussion Traumatic Brain Injuries
- Digestive Disorders: Bloating and Constipation Nausea and Acid Reflux GERD Swallowing Dysfunctions
- Women's and Men's Health Issues: Chronic Pelvic Pain Endometriosis Fibroids and Cysts Dysmenorrhea Bladder Incontinence Prostate Dysfunction Referred Testicular Pain Effects of Menopause
- Musculoskeletal Disorders: Somatic-Visceral Interactions Chronic Spinal Dysfunction Headaches and Migraines Carpal Tunnel Syndrome Peripheral Joint Pain Sciatica Neck Pain
- Pain Related to: Post-operative Scar Tissue Post-infection Scar Tissue
- Pediatric Issues: Constipation and Gastritis Persistent Vomiting Vesicoureteral Reflux Infant Colic
- Emotional Issues Anxiety and Depression Post-Traumatic Stress Disorder

PART 5

PSYCHOLOGICAL ASPECTS OF REHABILITATION

L et's say few words about the psychological aspects of rehabilitation. Plenty of neurological disorders and conditions with different severity, affecting an individual's functioning directly, can dramatically influence their lives. Significantly, such kinds of disabilities that lead to limited activities are connected with severe traumas and chronic diseases.

More often, clinical, physical, psychological, and socio-labor aspects of rehabilitation are distinguished. It is clear that without treating the underlying psychological processes and problems, it is much harder, or even impossible, to rehabilitate patients and people with acute traumas and chronicle disabilities. Simultaneously, the way we deal with complicated feelings about our illness or our loved ones is always individual, like the lines on our palms.

In many cases, to achieve successful psychological, social and occupational (labor) rehabilitation of patients, we, as a team, need to find a way to restore the physical work capacity and motor functions as much as possible. But if the patient's psychological status is not a concern and his psychological aspects (or field influence – like a divorce or grieving) constantly ignored, the whole rehabilitation process can become relatively slow and fragile or even will not bring the expected result. It can happen even if all the medical procedures and treatment went smoothly without complications.

As an example of such influence, there is the fact that physical rehabilitation not only increases physical workability but also significantly improves the psychological state of patients, even with severe disabilities. However, if a person's fear, high anxiety, and a rigid system of beliefs, the situation can differ. Different types of fears: fear for the heart dysfunction; fear of occurrence or intensification of back pain among patients with dorsopathy, etc., are correlating with the lack of personal motivation, fragile self-image, low self-esteem, and low self-efficacy, ignoring the need for self-participation in physical therapy classes. In case of depressive symptoms, the person feels fear of material (or occupational) work, which he believes is "harmful for his health." He is more likely to refuse to participate in a physical exercise program and seek a reason for disability. Such patients without proper psychological correction can't be involved in a physical rehabilitation program, or just their presence without active input practically reduces its effectiveness to zero.

In many cases, psychological factors, including low motivation rather than organic damage, can be the main reason for social and labor maladaptation. On the other side, return to work significantly speeds up and completes the process of psychological re-adaptation (restoration of the premorbid psychological status, adaptation to living conditions that have changed due to the illness.

That is why the system approach to rehabilitation, including the work with different specialists at the same time, can help the person to integrate himself into society, to find new meanings and goals, and diminish the consequences as a result of the disease. But this process is working vice versa: without personal client's motivation to change the current situation with his health and without his active position, even the resources and actions of the best team can fail. So in rehabilitation programs, the effectiveness of each component closely depends on the other ingredients. Inclusion into rehabilitation process and program of any critical part (clinical, psychological, physical, social and labor, etc.) and its direct effect, as a kind of synergy, indirectly significantly increases the effectiveness of other components whole mechanism.

Psychotherapy is a complex therapeutic influence system using a psychological approach on the patient's self, psyche, psychological processes, and it on the entire organism to eliminate painful symptoms and change attitudes toward oneself, one's condition, and the environment. Psychotherapy is a specific treatment method. Its effect is achieved by the quality of contact with the other person by the information and emotional charge it carries. Techniques and psychotherapy methods are widely used in the treatment and rehabilitation of mental disorders and a wide range of somatic conditions and play an essential role in rehabilitation processes.

It is essential to distinguish <u>two main types of psychotherapy</u>:
- nonspecific (psychotherapeutic approach)
- specific.

The psychotherapeutic approach is a nonspecific method of influencing the patient's psyche based on the medical deontology principles. Every doctor, regardless of specialty, needs to master this type of psychotherapy. This is a specific style and contact with the doctor, which influences the whole process of the treatment and can be supportive or damaging. The nonspecific conditions of psychotherapy include "doctor-patient," "nurse-patient" relations, "doctor-nurse" relations, and even the interior or atmosphere of the clinic. Nonspecific psychotherapy can start from the moment the patient enters a treatment institution: the comfortable atmosphere of the clinic, the beautiful interior, the polite and attentive way of communication between the patient and the staff and between each other, the efforts of the team to solve the patient's problems can create and generates the feeling of trust, safety, and hope for practical help. This is the start which is extremely important for the whole process of the treatment.

The fundamental purposes of the psychotherapeutic approach:

1. Reducing emotional tension. In reality, practically all our illnesses can create an emotional response in ourselves, especially anxiety, touching our safety issues, concerns about the outcome of the disease; worries about tests, procedures, treatment, consequences of the disease; further employment; and relationships with relatives. Patients' concerns can complicate treatment and the course of the disease. Information, clarification, distraction, nonverbal communication methods, and other ways of influence are used to reduce anxiety.
2. Mobilization of inner resources to fight the disease or trauma. In conversations, it is necessary to constantly underline that recovery can be slowed down or accelerated by own attitude toward the disease and treatment. A correct and adequate attitude toward the disease and its possible consequences is developed in communication with the patient and psychotherapist.
3. Increasing patient activity. This is a critical point. The patient needs to be involved in those acceptable activities for his condition as much as possible. It is necessary to eliminate the harmful effects of limitations of motor activities. For some patients to be by themselves with the disease or trauma can be extremely hard, and it is essential to support them to speak up about their worries and inner feelings. In this way, the mental activity is also stimulated: participation in the department's work and life or helping others can also be supportive for the patient.

Specific psychotherapy

There are plenty of specific methods and techniques, which are used in particular psychotherapy. In general, there are four main directions of specific psychotherapy:
- Psychodynamic
- Cognitive-behavioral
- Existential-humanistic
- Hypnosis and suggestive therapy.

Each of these orientations is based on specific personality theories and has its own logically connected psychotherapeutic influences system.

1. Psychodynamic - the founder of psychoanalysis is Sigmund Freud (Austria, 1856-1939). The term "psychodynamic" or "dynamic" implies consideration of a person's mental life in constant dynamics, movement, struggle, inner conflicts, and their impact on the personality. The main concepts studied within the psychoanalysis framework are the structure of a person's personality, stages of personality development, and mechanisms of psychological defense. Mainly it is a long-term therapy.

Short-term dynamic psychotherapy
The dynamic direction of psychotherapy has its origins in the classical psychoanalysis of Z. Freud. The most famous in the dynamic psychotherapy approach is Jung's analytical psychology, Adler's psychology, interpersonal psychotherapy (Sullivan), humanistic psychoanalysis (Fromm), etc.

Short-term dynamic psychotherapy has a less intensive character, unlike classical psychoanalysis, and can take the form of either psychotherapy focused on adequate self-esteem or relationship psychotherapy which is aimed at psychological support of the patient in difficult psychological situations. The therapy goals are similar to those of classical analysis (resolution of unconscious conflict), but the main emphasis is on everyday reality.

2. Cognitive-behavioral psychotherapy is fundamentally different from the psychodynamic approach. Psychotherapy focused on changing beliefs, attitudes, ways of thinking, and behavior of the person and learning the new skills. Behavior is understood as a totality of the body's reactions to environmental influences and certain stimuli, and a person is viewed as a carrier of certain forms of behavior. The central problem of behaviorism is learning (teaching), i.e., the acquisition of

individual experience. The cognitive-behavioral trend includes the following methods:
- Behavioral psychotherapy
- Cognitive psychotherapy
- Rational-emotive psychotherapy
- Rational psychotherapy.

3. Existential-humanistic - This direction is very heterogeneous and includes a variety of psychotherapeutic schools united by a general approach to considering the purposes of psychotherapy and ways to achieve them. Humanistic psychology views the personality as a unique, holistic system, which cannot be understood through individual manifestations and components. It is the holistic approach to the person that has become one of the fundamental tenets of humanistic psychology. The main task is to create conditions conducive to new experiences in which the patient changes his or her Self-esteem in a positive direction. The main directions here are Gestalt Therapy, Positive Therapy, etc.

4. Hypnosis and suggestive methods - Suggestive therapy is a form of psychotherapy in which the elimination of bodily and mental disorders is achieved by using the suggestion in the form of a verbal message describing the state to be completed. There is a targeted influence on functional disorders, autonomic disorders, conditions of tension, pain, and many others. Suggestive therapy includes hypnosis, suggestion, and auto-training.

Hypnosis is a particular state of consciousness that occurs under the influence of directed psychological impact, which differs from both sleep and wakefulness and is accompanied by a significant increase in sensitivity to specifically directed psychological factors with a sharp decrease in sensitivity to the action of all other environmental factors.

Therapeutic suggestions are constructed considering the patient's unique features, specificity of symptomatology, and the character of a course of illness. Suggestion formulas should be short and specific.

Also, there are classifications of psychotherapy according to the main focus:
- Problem-oriented psychotherapy (focused on a specific problem with which the patient consults a psychotherapist)
- Personality-oriented psychotherapy (focused on the root cause of the disorder, lying in the personality structure).

According to the number of people with whom the psychotherapist works simultaneously, there are a present individual or group therapy.

So, you see plenty of ways to work with psychological aspects, and it is important to find what works for you.

The mechanisms of psychotherapy's therapeutic effect include the following: touching and expressing the sphere of emotions, facilitation of emotional release, understanding ourselves, obtaining information, strengthening the patient's belief in recovery or the best adjustment, accumulating positive experiences and training Self-support and other individual aspects.

Stages of psychotherapy

Psychotherapeutic intervention always passes through several stages of the psychotherapist-patient relationships. However, psychotherapy can end with positive results for the patient at the final stage and any intermediate steps. Those steps are:

1. Establishment of contact and achievement of compatibility (a psychologically comfortable, trusting atmosphere of interpersonal interaction is formed, which is favorable for cooperation).
2. Clarification of the problem (the primary collection of information and allocation of the most significant issues, the psychotherapist's and, to some extent, the patient's understanding of the causes, mechanisms of emotional and behavioral formation disorders, illnesses, or trauma.
3. Identifying psychotherapeutic targets and formulating the main problems.
4. Application of specific methods and techniques (the most time-consuming process).
5. Adjustment and evaluation of whether psychotherapy has changed the patient's behavior and life situation and the activation of the patient's independent activity or not.
6. Ending the course of psychotherapy.

Contraindications for psychotherapy:

1. Acute psychotic conditions
2. High probability of developing a seizure syndrome
3. Severe brain organic syndrome, dementia
4. Presence of decompensated somatic diseases (here can be used supportive therapy).

Following a holistic perspective on a human being, there is no doubt that the first stage of this traumatic experience (acute trauma) is connected with survival purposes. It is acute stress for the human and his body on different levels. Depending on the stress factor, there are two main types of stress: physiological (mainly body reactions) and psychological. Psychological stress can be subdivided into informational and emotional, which develops in situations of threat or danger.

Different incidents can affect everyone in one way or another, but the range of possible reactions and emotions is extensive. Many people feel shocked, disoriented, or unaware of what is happening. They can feel anxiety, pain, fear, or can be numb or apathetic, but this is mainly about short-term reactions, which can be mild or more acute and severe according to their intensity. But the main long-term psychological reactions are postponed till the moment when body functions are more or less stabilized.

All of them connected with trauma. There are many additional factors of the personal reactions, including:
1. the nature and severity of the event experienced;
2. traumatic events experienced in the past;
3. presence of outside support in life;
4. previous experience of dealing with traumas;
5. physical health;
6. mental health issues (including past history and family history);
7. age (for example, children of different age groups react differently).

Our stress reactions are nonspecific, stressors cause a one-type (nonspecific) response of the body, which is known as the **general adaptation syndrome (GAS),** which means that the body works automatically to prevent the damage and stabilize the functions. Acute stress-response of the body is mainly connected with physiological adjustment to the body's changes. This is the first stage of stress, known as the <u>alarm reaction of anxiety and resource mobilization</u>. In this phase, the adaptation of the organism to new conditions begins. At this stage, the person copes with the load by means of functional mobilization of the body's corresponding organs and systems, without structural rearrangements.

In the second phase, which is known as a <u>phase of resistance</u>, all the body's parameters out of equilibrium in the first phase are stabilized and fixed at a new level. Adaptation reserves are intensively overdrawn. The duration of the resistance depends on the organism's innate adaptive capacity and the stressor's strength.

This is the period when professional medical treatment is crucial. An emotionally stable environment, providing clear information and support, can also play a critical role in stabilizing the situation and decreasing the later consequences of a traumatic experience.

If the stressful situation continues to persist, the third phase of stress - exhaustion - occurs since humans' abilities to adapt is not limitless. Psychological reactions and conditions play a vital role during this phase, and with professional support, they can be changed. Everyone has strengths and abilities that help them cope with the challenges of life. However, some people can be more vulnerable in a crisis and may need additional help, provided as soon as possible.

Psychological rehabilitation as an aspect of medical rehabilitation.
Medical and psychological rehabilitation is an integral component of the rehabilitation of patients, especially with a disability. Without psychological methods, it is impossible to achieve successful rehabilitation in many cases. Or, let's say the complex of rehabilitative methods and different ways of working with the patient (or client) can be much more effective than just medical treatment.

Misunderstanding, difficulties in connection, unresolved personal psychological issues and existential perspectives, low resources, fears of physical exertion in long-term in-patient treatment, lack of motivation to overcome the disease and its consequences, different forms of resistance, low adherence of patients to participate in medical rehabilitation programs, high and failing expectations, helplessness and hopelessness, anxiety, fears, and depression - all those things can influence dramatically on the outcome and client's readiness to struggle and readiness to go on.

Quite often, the honest dialogue between the doctor and the patient with the support, clear messages, essential helpful information, the readiness for discussion, and the possibility to express the feelings is already a massive part of the treatment and the start of rehabilitation the person.

In addition to the primary treatment, psychotherapy or different types of psychological help can be provided during the period of medical treatment and rehabilitation and can include several primary forms:
• crisis intervention;
• psychological counseling;
• psychological correction;

- psychotherapy;
- psychological rehabilitation;
- psychological training.

Crisis intervention – is emergency psychological aid to individuals in crisis (victims of war conflicts, violence, natural disasters, catastrophes; acute traumatic experience, people with losses and acute grieving, etc.) aimed at preventing the development of mental disorders and behavioral disorders.

Psychological counseling focuses on helping the client resolve a particular problem situation and provides an opportunity to expand his understanding of various aspects of his personality and the social environment.

Psychological correction is a directed psychological impact on specific mental structures to ensure the individual's full development and functioning.

Psychotherapy aims to improve the mental state of the person with mental or behavioral disorders or without them, focusing not just on the elimination of the symptoms of these disorders by methods of psychological influence, but mainly in a life-quality and adaptation to the current environment. It can be short-term and long-term, depending on the focus of work and problems, which the client wants to explore or resolve.

Psychological rehabilitation - assistance to the patient/client, aimed at restoring his abilities as fully as possible, improving his quality of life, improving social adaptation, integration into society, and preventing the development of permanent personality disorders and negative changes in his lifestyle.

The psychological training goal is to support personal growth and develop the necessary psychological and behavioral skills: coping with stress, resolving conflicts, making decisions, etc.

Psychological aid can be provided both individually and in groups (family or group therapy) and within an entire organization (organizational consultation). There are no rigid boundaries between various kinds of psychological aid. It concerns, first of all, psychological consultation, psychological correction, and psychotherapy. Today, there is a significant number of directions in psychological support and therapy: Psychoanalysis, Behavioral and Cognitive behavioral therapy (CBT), Existential psychotherapy, Rational-emotional therapy, Gestalt therapy, Art-therapy, and others. Each of them is defined by what is put forward as the basic reason for the client's psychological problems through the essential characteristics of a healthy, adapted personality. During the first meeting with the counselor/therapist with the client, all those questions and focuses for work, formats, and possible results can be discussed in detail, and then the client can make up his mind about his interest in work.

It is impossible to achieve successful rehabilitation without psychological methods, the ultimate goal of rehabilitation in some cases. At the same time, for any specialist, who is providing psychological support and psychotherapy, it's vital to follow the main ethical rules:

- respect the right of people to make their own decisions;
- make it clear that even if they refuse to apply for help now, they may ask for it in the future;
- be honest and worthy of trust;
- be opened and flexible according to the need of every particular person;
- respect confidentiality and prevent the unwarranted disseminate the client's (patient's) personal information;
- keep in mind and follow an appropriate manner according to the local culture, age, and gender characteristics;
- don't make false promises or provide incorrect information;
- don't exaggerate the knowledge and skills;
- don't force people to accept the help, using an intrusive "should."

It's important to keep in mind that medical treatment aimed at medico-psychological rehabilitation of patients and people with disabilities does not always lead to psychological re-adaptation). Sometimes, it can be an ongoing process of support and slow restoration of patients' status. Feel free to ask. For clients, it's important to know about the method, which will be provided, specific frames, quantity (when it's possible) of the sessions, format. That can be individual or group sessions, working with the family or family members, rules, which can establish a relationship between the therapist and the client and create a safe atmosphere for the treatment purposes.

For practical purposes, we can distinguish two main categories of persons with the potential need of psychological rehabilitation:

1) Group of people, patients, and clients with acute medical problems, connected with a real threat to the person's life and well-being (for example, car accident). Acute trauma arises suddenly, causing well-defined personal-psychological reactions to the disease or the details of traumatic experience with mainly neurotic responses and issues around adjustment to the life-threatening changes and all kinds of limitations.
2) Group of people, patients, and clients whose medical problems are connected with progressive chronic illnesses, early traumas, or congenital pathology. Personal-psychological reactions are less visible, unnoticed, and much more stable, and can form personal pathological patterns if it starts from early childhood.

Inadequate psychological reactions to illness and pathological development of the personality become a severe barrier to rehabilitation. So for conducting psychological rehabilitation, it is important to know:
- Unsatisfied critical needs here-and-now;
- Preliminary psychological status of patient/client (unresolved issues, stress-situations, personal traits, coping mechanisms, personal experience in solving life problems, and the primary way of dealing with them);
- System of support (who, what, how – and details of the close environment and the quality of connection);
- Need in medical, psychiatric support and treatment;
- Understanding of the nature of psychological and body changes at the different stages of the disease, diagnostics, and treatment;
- Factors of psychological re-adaptation.

We all are humans. So we need to be treated by humans. And this is a hugely important focus of medical work and patient's (or his family member's) communication with medical providers. A person needs special attention from doctors and clinical psychologists during the phase of informing about diagnosis, diagnostic procedures, plan of the treatment, and possible prognosis when understanding the essence of the disease just starts.

Of course, all situations connected with disability or trauma, or illness are unique and individual. But at the same time, **there are some common moments.**

What happens if your child is disabled?
Every child, every person is entitled to special care and assistance from our society. But there are children with varying degrees of disability whose physical and mental condition requires increased attention from parents.

In general, the concept of a "disabled child" can be divided into two categories. <u>One group of children with disabilities in children with congenital abnormalities</u> of various sensory organs and physical disabilities or mentally retarded children. Limitations can be different and severe. At the same time, numerous studies have shown that the creative potential of such children is enormous. Their talents represent significant cultural values. And the effect of harmonious personal development and successful adaptation in society is beneficial to the children's health. We never know precisely the child's full potential and need to start working in the situations with all those limitations of "knowing" in uncertain cases. But it is important to do everything we can in those situations.

Another group of children is those who became disabled as a result of an extended illness or trauma. Upbringing and developing such children is a severe pedagogical and medical problem, and of course, the issue of rehabilitation.

It is well known that to successfully solve any life problem or difficult situation; it is necessary to understand it. This is why parents need to know specific psychological recommendations that will effectively and steadfastly overcome life's difficulties.

Family is a system. It is a particular system with its inner world, lows, norms, communication and relationship quality, quality of connection and care, hierarchy, and role models. A child's disability, more often than not, becomes the cause of deep and prolonged social maladaptation of the entire family. Indeed, raising a child with developmental disabilities, regardless of the nature and timing of their illness or injury, changes and often disrupts the whole normal rhythm of family life. The discovery of a child's defect developmental defect and confirmation of disability almost always causes severe stressful conditions, and the family finds itself in a psychologically difficult situation.

Parents despair, can be desperate and cry; some carry the pain within them, stop grieving, not allowing themselves to feel, becoming detached or irritated or even aggressive and confronting. Parents of a child with a disability may completely alienate themselves from friends, acquaintances, and often from relatives. This is a time of pain, which must be endured, a time of sorrow that must be poured out. Only by experiencing grief can a person look at the situation calmly to approach the solution more constructively. So it means every time we are faced with the **situation of loss,** we need to grieve.

The whole dynamic of the family can be changed if the child is disabled. There are different types of scenarios that could have a place with different outcomes. Codependency, tension, complementary roles, limited resources, emotional, physical, and financial, passive-aggressive patterns can become a part of the family's reality. It can influence a lot on the child's rehabilitation process because all family members can require dissatisfaction and have to deal with the high level of frustration. Sometimes the traumatic event can become so powerful that the whole family system can fall apart and partners divorce.

Dealing with marriage problems, family and children, mainly the specialists underline those typical reactions to stress connected with the disease or even disability of the child, including denial, sadness, and anger.

Psychologists distinguish four phases of the psychological attitude and forming the position towards a disabled child.

The first phase - "shock", is characterized by the state of confusion of parents, helplessness, fear, and the occurrence of a feeling of their inferiority.

The second phase, – is "inadequate attitude towards the defect," characterized by negativism and denial of the diagnosis, which is a peculiar defensive reaction.

The third phase – is "partial realization of the child's defect," accompanied by feelings of "chronic sadness" or chronic grieving. This is a complex ongoing process of accepting the fact that the child is constantly dependent on the parent/parents, and the child's needs will require the process of parent's serving.

The fourth phase is the beginning of the social-psychological adaptation of all family members, acceptance of the defect and disability, establishing good relations with specialists, and good adherence to their recommendations.

Unfortunately, not all mothers and fathers in families with a disabled child can cope with the situation; family and personal problems can become overwhelming. They have difficulty coming to the right decision and gaining a future life perspective. They need professional support.

A family with a disabled child suffers from medical, economic, social, and psychological problems, leading to a deterioration in the quality of their life and family and personal problems; the family can become "dysfunctional" for all the family system members. Such cases include the following situations: isolate themselves, not accepting help from outside and rejecting the support, not following the restrictions or recommendations, losing the balance between their personal goals and care, and lose the meaning of life.

Help from relatives and friends can be optional. But when relatives and acquaintances learn about the severe trauma or an illness of the child, they also experience psychological stress with different reactions and severity. Some relatives and friends begin to avoid meetings because they fear their feelings and emotions and those of the child's parents. It is challenging for the parents of the spouses (grandparents).

Not knowing how to help and being afraid to be tactless, relatives and acquaintances sometimes prefer to keep silent and ignore the situation, which complicates the parents' concern with a disabled child. This is especially true for mentally retarded children, who attract unhealthy curiosity and constant questioning by people, acquaintances, and strangers. All this puts a heavy burden on the parents. It is difficult to get used to the idea that your child is "different". Fear for the future of their child, confusion, ignorance of the psychological peculiarities of upbringing, a sense of shame that "gave birth to an inferior child," lead to the fact that parents often shut themselves off from relatives, friends, and acquaintances, preferring to grieve alone

To diminish the amount of pressure, everyone has to think about his or her relationship with the child and his or her parents and has to determine the amount of support that is ready to provide without "feeling a victim". The best way will be to speak openly about those limitations to check the expectations.

As a reaction to stress, children with acute trauma can behave regressively: go back to the pacifier, to diapers, suck their thumb, have nightmares in their sleep, children may do less well at games, studies, complain of headaches and stomachaches. Pay attention to those symptoms; quite often, these children are not "misbehaving" - they are afraid and need to reestablish the safety.

Children's fears are often associated with sleep, a necessary function of which is to "digest" all the experiences of the day. Those people whose sleep has been affected by some trauma subsequently complain of a more significant number of psychological and physiological problems. It is crucial to ensure sufficient and good sleep.

Here are some tips:
Take care of clear boundaries about the time and place of sleep, good conditions for rest (clean bed, pleasant room temperature, bedtime story, use humor), try to stick to a routine (hygiene, meals, etc.).

Have a quiet time together, plan and pack things together for tomorrow (clothes, school tasks, etc.)

Try to relax the child, invite him to fall asleep to soothing music, talk to him about how the day went; if the child still has trouble falling asleep, let him get out of bed, have a little snack, drink warm milk.

Spend more time together; allow them to be more dependent on you in the first weeks after a trauma. Physical contact, hugs are very soothing for children who have been through a stressful situation.

Give children the opportunity to express themselves in games, drawing, sculpting, drama (play a puppet theater, for example). Children, especially very young children, express themselves better through play rather than with words. This promotes the effective processing of experiences.

Notice and try to understand precisely child's feelings. Do not rely on your assumptions that he is less afraid than he seems, or conversely, do not assume that the child does not understand that something is going on. Take your child's fears seriously. Don't try to convince him that he is not afraid.

Try to react calmly. Harsh treatment, much less shouting or scolding, will only increase the child's fears: a warm, loving look, a calm voice; it is important to caress the child, hug him or her, encourage the child to go on as usual.

Ensure that the child is not afraid to ask questions and answer the child's questions directly, but in a way that is appropriate to his level and age. Do not give unnecessary information that the child has not asked for.

Try to keep the routine (eating, studying, playing, sleeping) as much as possible to restore the child's sense of security and help her get back to her way. This has a calming effect on children.

If you must be away for a while, keep in touch with the children, make sure they know where you are going, how long you will be gone, and try to return at the promised time.

That advice can help your child, and you keep the connection and cope with the difficult situation.

In a disability, living with a child with a disability is always difficult, but some periods are tough to deal with psychologically. Those periods, from a psychological view, are:

1. The moment and the following period of discovering, especially by doctors and medical practitioners, of the child's developmental disorder or disability or any other serious issue. This is a period of occurrence of fears and uncertainty in the child's upbringing, experiencing hopelessness and helplessness of the situation.

2. Senior preschool age of the child (5-7 years old) – Parent's fears about the child's ability to study in a regular school and child's reactions towards this point.

3. Teenage period (13-15 years old) – growing of self and the normal process of separation creates a new awareness of his or her disability. Problems of stigma emerge. Intensive emotional and behavioral reactions can be part of the process. The child experiences a psychophysiological and psychosocial age crisis associated with accelerated and uneven maturation of the musculoskeletal, cardiovascular and sexual systems, the desire to communicate with peers, and self-assertion. The child actively develops self-esteem and self-awareness. New questions, new solutions, new reactions are part of the crisis. Forming of Self-image can lead to difficulties in establishing contacts with peers and the opposite sex. Isolation of the family from society can also be an issue. In this challenging period, the child gradually becomes aware that they are not different from everyone else. The family members crisis, associated with adolescence, is added with the "middle-life crisis" of the parents, the "crisis of the age of forty." By this age, people reach specific stability of social and professional position, gain confidence in the future, summarize their lives, and enter maturity; there are changes in physiology. All those aspects can rearrange the conflicts in the parent-child relationship.

4. High school age (15-17 years old) –questions and difficulties for parents in determining and getting a profession and further employment of the growing child, his own decisions about it, about the family, sexual questions. Parent's fears about their death and disability or illness, intrapersonal discord in the family also can be present.

It should be noted that not every family goes through all four crises. Some families can "stop" at the second crisis - in the case if the child has a complicated developmental pathology or medical issue (profound mental retardation, severe cerebral palsy, multiple disabilities, etc.). In this case, the child does not study at all, and for parents, the central role is caregiver care. In other families (for example, if the child has a somatic illness), the second crisis passes without much complication, i.e., the child starts school and learns. Later, difficulties of other periods (the third and fourth) can appear.

Specialists working with such a family (social workers, pedagogical psychologists) need to know the specifics of these crises in a family with a child with a disability and provide the necessary social and psychological support and care.

What has to be done?

Being lonely and dealing with all those difficulties is a huge problem. In a crisis, it is necessary to pay attention, not to leave them alone. Simultaneously, it is important to give the space and balance the "presence and freedom" according to the moment and according to the needs, to be flexible enough without being demanding. The person with limitations and disablement must have someone nearby, a close relative or friend, or the medical staff and caregivers. In this case, psychologists or those parents who have a child with a similar pathology or developmental disability can be a support to help parents to overcome the difficult period.

The method of helping children overcome fears involves acknowledging the existence of these fears in children and trying to reassure them, encourage them, and give them confidence. Noticing, understanding, and saying aloud what the child is feeling, naming them helps children understand themselves and begin coping with these feelings.

Young children are entirely dependent on their parents. They feel what their parents feel and react accordingly. If the adult is calm, confident, the child will feel safe. The panic of the adult is transmitted to the child immediately. This is why it is so important that parents can help themselves to calm down to create the best behavioral model for the child, understanding and distinguishing between their feelings and the child's feelings.

Children will need more support, reassurance to reestablish the sense of safety and security. Speak to them in a language they understand and don't assume they are too young to understand what is going on. They also need the information, not just you. Unnaturally trying to restore a child's sense of safety is ineffective. Don't tell the child "don't worry" because worry is natural in such situations, so don't give false promises. Tell your child that you will be with them. Nevertheless, adults do everything they can to keep children safe.

Invite the child to talk to you or friends about their experiences, feelings, and thoughts. This helps with the panic, fears, and anxiety associated with experiencing stress. Help your child regain confidence in the future by making plans together for the next week and the next month, even the plans for short periods.

Sometimes we can't change reality completely. But still, we can change a lot. Parents can look at the situation from a different perspective as an opportunity to revise their lives, values, and attitudes. To gather their strength and will and love the child for who he is; live together with him, give him warmth, care, and attention, enjoy life and help other mothers and fathers with the same problems find their peace of mind.

In difficult life situations, at least, there are always three options:
1. Leave everything as it is, or change something;
2. Change our behavior, habits, views, attitudes, or change the circumstances in which the problem arose;
3. If it is impossible to change the circumstances, it is possible to change the attitude to the circumstances or to accept them as a necessary given. As a lesson to be passed, as a catalyst of inner-personal growth and reviling the resources and possibilities, something positive is contained in what is still perceived as negative.

Recommendations for parents with children with disabilities:
1. Do your grieving work alone, with support, or with the specialist. Allow yourself to have feelings and to express them, not just thoughts.
2. Believe in your child; never feel sorry for a child because he or she is different.
3. Give your child your love and attention, but don't forget that other family members need them, too. Organize your life so that no one in the family feels like a "victim, by giving up their personal life.
4. Try not only to protect your child from everything and all the problems you have, from responsibilities and difficulties. Solve all things together with him, involved in the family life according to his age and potential.
5. Allow your child autonomy of actions and decision-making and support the growths and new skills, even if sometimes it seems easier to make everything on your own.

6. Watch how you look and behave, pay attention to your reactions; your child is learning from you the most.
7. Don't be afraid to say "no" to your child if you think his or her demands are excessive.
8. Talk to your child more often. Remember that neither television, or computer, or phone can replace you and actual contact.
9. Think about limitations about your child's interactions with peers; remember that they are changing.
10. Allow him to meet friends, invite them to visit.
11. Use the advice of teachers and psychologists more often.
12. Read more, and not only special literature, get a chance to see what is new and what is possible.
13. Communicate with families who have disabled children. Pass on your experience and share your own experience and adapt to the experiences of others.
14. Work with guilt and shame. Don't beat yourself up with recriminations. The fact that you have a sick child is not your fault!
15. Remember that someday your child will grow up and have to live on their own. Prepare him for his future life by talking to him about it and supporting his skills.

What is going on when you are an adult and have the problem of severe trauma or disability?

It is also a tremendous change for every person and enormous stress. Here is a place for Grief and Loss psychological reactions. The patient learns from the doctor and medical team and Google and relatives and friends about this particular illness. He becomes more and more aware of the severity of this disease, which threatens his well-being and life itself, requiring difficult-to-tolerate treatment (surgery, chemotherapy, and prolonged bed rest). This causes the patient anxiety and fear for life and health, gloomy but intense, thousands of thoughts about the future and personal issues, leading to depression, fear of possible disability, a sense of the collapse of one's career, and sometimes life. Pain, weakness, physical discomfort exacerbates the patient's reaction to the mental trauma, the role of which is a severe and dangerous illness.

The importance of understanding personal reactions and the possibility to get professional help, if needed, can't be overestimated. Everything is possible to be present: both adequate and pathological emotional reactions to illness and treatment, as well as their associated actual and/or expected consequences.

There are described and distinguished several types oa personal reactions connected with disease: some are normal, and few are pathological. It is important to determine them to get professional help if needed before they become fixed patterns. It is normal to have emotional reactions to trauma and disease, and it is normal to grieve when we are ill.

Types of personal reactions to the disease are qualified as usual, if:
- The patient's behavior, experience, and ideas about the illness correspond to the information received from the doctor about the severity of the disease and treatment
- The patient is following the medical regime and limitations, taking part in the process of the treatment and rehabilitation;
- The patient is present with his emotional state but being able to control his emotions.

Sometimes more strong or prolonged reactions to the disease can be seen as neurotic reactions (phobic, anxiety disorders, etc.) or as reactions to severe stress, including adaptation problems. In some other cases, reactions to the disease can be much stronger. They can influence the person's emotional state, prognosis, position towards the treatment and rehabilitation and create many doctor-patient complacence difficulties. There are many different types and descriptions of psychological reactions on trauma or disease, which are creating the special patterns of behavior or the person and can influence his activity and the process of recovering. Following few types of psychopathological personality reactions to the illness may need special correction and treatment:

- **Anosognosic reaction** - There is a denial of the illness with disregard of treatment recommendations and gross violations of the medical regime. It occurs more often in male patients than in female ones. In oncology, it is observed much more often than in somatic diseases and physical traumas.

- **Phobic reaction – is** present with high intensity and constant phobias, fear of recurrent stroke, tumor metastases, recurrence of a disease, sudden death.

- **Depressive (anxious-depressive) reaction** - manifested by a lowered mood, pessimistic estimation of the future and perspectives, constant internal tension, low energy and decreased life functions, sleeping problems, different aches.

- **Somatized, depressive-hypochondriac reaction)** - characterized by a constant, chronic, and evident overestimation of the severity of his condition and fixed attention on his health, ignoring other life focuses.

- **Hysterical reaction** - Observed as Self-centeredness, demonstrativeness, striving to attract others' attention and elicit sympathy, high level of emotional instability and lability, quickly bursting into tears or becoming irritated and angry.

There are different types of psychotherapy and psychological correction that can be useful for those clients to help them join the rehabilitation process with a more active position. That is why it is important to know about them.

The above psychological reactions are characteristic of premorbid mentally healthy individuals. Such cases, where somatic disease develops in the preliminary pathological background (patients with chronic alcoholism, drug abuse, chronicle diseases, vascular and traumatic diseases of the brain, mental disorders, etc.) require the attending psychiatrist, who can add and recommend additional treatment to the psychotherapy.

Usually, in few weeks after starting the disease (in mild cases) or after several months (in more severe cases or illnesses with disability), the personal reactions to the disease and its consequences are gradually disappearing. This is a Grief and Loss inner individual work period, which is naturally moving through all stages. The five stages of grief are denial, anger, bargaining, depression, and acceptance. In a period of 6 to 12 months from the start of the illness or physical trauma, in most cases, psychological re-adaptation to life can be formed, and acceptance means new adaptation, new adjustment of the person to the changed conditions life. It can often be a completely different life, with further limitations and unknown possibilities and options.

The rest of the patients with severe trauma, disablement, development of oncological, somatic, or neurological illnesses can still feel difficulties to tolerate treatment. Even with stable bodily conditions, they can aggravate, consolidate, and finally form neurotic adaptation. Those forms can include depressive and anxiety disorders, maladaptive behavior patterns can be developed and fixed the pathological personality development. Those "retreats into illnesses" narrow the range of interests (focusing only on their health's problems), disruption of social ties and social self-isolation, rent attitudes, and chronicle depression.

Factors affecting the process of psychological rehabilitation:

The main factors that impede the rehabilitation process in patients with somatic diseases are different types of preliminary mental disorders. First of all, such as depressive, somatic symptom disorder (SSD), formerly known as "somatization disorder" or "somatoform disorder," phobic disorders and personality disorders.

One of the most critical risk factors, influencing and even determining the personal reaction to the illness and the following disability, especially in somatic chronicle diseases, are the main features of patients' personality. Individuals with anxious elements of the character, mistrustfulness, psychological inflexibility, as a rule, can much more often create a phobic or hypochondriac reaction to the illness.

Some other individuals who, even before the traumatic experience with the disease, are inclined to react to life's difficulties of life with despair, depressed mood, disbelief in the possibility of change, negatively oriented with black-and-white view on the current situation and on the world in general can easier respond to the disease with a depressive reaction and even self-harm reactions.

At the same time, the degree of harmony in the structure of the personality, the presence of self-knowledge of the person, openness to emotional reactions, flexibility, ability to tolerate different stressors and positive coping mechanisms, acceptance of personal limitations without additional victimizing themselves (like the belief that "the whole world is against me", "it's only my fault") can be an important support for recovering.

Personal psychotherapy and self-care habits, premorbid stability to psychologically traumatic situations, correlate with the frequency and severity of psychopathological reactions to the disease. It decreases it\s intensity and disorganized influence on the person. It's never too late. If you are interested in change, awareness, and creating new forms of attitude and behavior towards life events, exploring new strategies and ways of satisfying important needs, psychotherapy can be quite helpful. Besides, there are plenty of ways to get a unique experience and new knowledge about psychological aspects and their rehabilitation and recovery role.

So, summarizing all above, we see that patients' resources and coping strategies greatly influence psychological adaptation to the disease.

The main therapeutic focuses are:
- Meditation
- Relaxation techniques
- Self-support concept
- Grief-and-Loss work, when it's necessary
- Existential perspective with new orienteers and tasks
- Working with anger

- Anxiety and depression
- Attitude towards the disease and life, "victims" position versa active position
- Ability to choose which way to go, even with limitations
- Harmony and stability
- Discovering new potential and restructure of Self and Self-images
- Re-integration in relationship with actual important needs
- Social presence.

The positive psychological impact on the patients and the favorable dynamics of somatic condition has therapeutic exercises, focusing on Self-support, strengthening the client's confidence in the recovery, or stabilizing his situation.

It's pretty important to recognize the patterns and negative thinking habits, which can stop and sabotage the process of recovering. The graduate changing of strict medical regime, adding physical exercises, and psychological support can help eliminate anxiety about health concerns and different types of fears, including the fear of physical exertion.

The family plays a vital role in providing emotional support and comprehensive assistance to the patient and disabled person. Quite often, the person's main psychological difficulties and expressed directly to the family members can also be quite traumatic. In those cases, the family members' psychological support becomes an important focus and priority. The whole situation of the serious illness of a beloved one is also tough to accept and demands a personal grieving process and time to accept. Simultaneously, too much care and support of a disabled or ill person, doing everything for him without any boundaries can easily create tension and conflicts in the family field, leading to burn-out syndrome. That is why it's important not only to "serve above self" but to be informed about the main symptoms of burn-out syndrome and get all the information about possible family support and available resources.

Negative psychological effects

In general, touching the age aspect, young patients react more expressively and acutely to the disease and trauma, especially if that poses a threat of disability in the nearest future. Of course, it's a vast and tremendous loss for every person you are young and active. So, for teenagers and young people, at the height of their health and vitality, there is a considerable risk of depressive, self-harm reactions, and even suicidal tendencies, which shouldn't be ignored. When you are so young, illness and injury are usually not present in the person's inner world. The sudden development of dangerous diseases or suffering from a severe physical injury is perceived as a catastrophe.

 Behavioral changes can be dramatic: total isolation from friends and family members, complete silence and defensive mechanisms, acute and prolonged protest reactions, anger expression, and even violence towards others. Psychological suffering and grieving have personal own unique style. That is why psychological support and counseling can't be "general"; it's an individual process of reconstructing the life and dealing with new reality with the specialist's help.

Elderly patients tend to view their illnesses as a part of life's reality and are more ready to deal with this process, being more mature and mainly having a history of ups-and-downs in their own lives. But of course, many other factors can influence the process of dealing with severe disease, entirely personal and unique.

Psychological rehabilitation is a part of systemic work. It is conducted primarily by physicians and clinical psychologists in the hospital. In close cooperation with other specialists, clinical psychologists, therapists, or even psychiatrists, if needed, can participate in a comprehensive rehabilitation program.

The main phases (tasks) of psychological rehabilitation include the following:
1. **Psychological diagnosic procedures and processes** should be conducted as early as possible, allowing the specialists to identify patients who need psychological support and correction in the early stages, patients with a primary need for rehabilitation. They need to be monitored and observed during the process of the treatment. They can get psychologically corrective treatment also from the beginning to get better results in future recovering.

2. **Psychological correction and therapy:**
   - psychological support (the first days of the illness, hospitalization, emergency department, if needed; the process of informing the patient about his diagnosis, complications, especially when the disease is severe and treatment is long-term; before and after surgery or painful and uncomfortable diagnostic procedures, before discharge from hospital, etc.);
   - forming of working compliance between medical providers and the patient, creating the dialog;
   - helping the person to develop adequate personal reactions to the disease;

- expression in a safe atmosphere personal feelings (anger, sadness, fear, anxiety, possible joy), grief and loss reactions, informing about the stages and assimilating the current moment;
- exploring the most important needs of the person;
- support in the process of awareness of the current situation,
- increase of adherence to treatment;
- support of active participation in rehabilitation programs;
- discussing the issues around the possibility to return to work (or study) in time, actions to restorey their role in the family, social, and work environment.

Psychological rehabilitation is quite individual and specific for every client and every patient in his particular life period, age, personality, and environment. A complicated analysis of those factors and their influence on the patient's recovery process can be preventive measure for the patient's negative attitude towards his treatment and can see risk factors in advance.

Methods of psychological rehabilitation are different, but the focus and content of this therapy are determined by the specific condition of the patient, his psychological state and are oriented around his acute needs and the tasks to be solved at different rehabilitation stages. Mainly it's dialogical therapy, which is conducted through confidential conversations. It is crucial to meet the person he is with his experience, not just following the protocol. To be heard and to be visible with all mixed feelings, thoughts, and imaginations; to share in a safe atmosphere what is important for now, meet with suppressed emotions and fears, and meet with helplessness and hopelessness. Also, to reassure the right to react to the current reality – all those critical moments are part of a therapeutic relationship. Such kind of healing contact is already the start for a change of the person. When it is possible to share what is going on inside the person, to live with this experience for a while, being not alone, but without intrusion; then it is possible to find the inner support and discover the potential and resources which every person has inside and to get the unique position and confidence back. It is then possible to discuss what can be done, for now, the options and limitations, and the best ways to cope with this situation and problem.

The process of therapy is flexible, so what is vital for here-and-now can be the main focus: the essence of the disease and the importance of the ongoing treatment measures, psychological preparation before the surgery, or any dangerous, difficult, frightening, or painful diagnostic procedure, the beginning of hard-to-tolerate treatment (such as chemotherapy), questions about the future ability to work and possible limitations and many others...

It is necessary to draw the patient's attention to positive (even if small) changes in their bodies during treatment. All the preliminary personal problems and traumatic experiences from childhood can arise during this period of dealing with disease, so it will be important to pay attention to them in therapy or counseling.

In psychological rehabilitation, various psycho-relaxation techniques are commonly used when patients are taught self- muscular and psychological relaxation techniques and a special way of breezing. The formula describes heaviness or lightness in separate parts of the body and slowly in the whole body. Those methods are effective self-supportive measures.

Psychological preparation for discharge is another psychological rehabilitation phase, so all the necessary information about long-term therapy, group, and individual counseling, support groups, hot-telephone numbers for crisis intervention, books, and materials should be provided. This is an important support for the person and his family members. The lack of a responsible attitude often leads to the fact that some of his fears can come back after the patient is discharged. Clarity of medical providers and psychologists in this sphere can prevent the negative impact of losing outside structure and support in the hospital and create useless self-limitations, slowing down rehabilitation.

Psychological support is also required before returning to work (study). The appropriate psychotherapeutic climate, the prevention of traumatic experience connected with medical providers' mistakes ("iatrogenies" - non-clarity, stigma, devaluations, actions, etc.) must be available and provided all times by all medical team.

Besides, psychological counseling and therapy can be provided for family members, especially spouses/partners of the patient, children, if needed, and other family members in the patient's immediate environment. Informational and psychological support will include the current situation, difficulties, and ways to overcome them, possible consequences, and what can be done. It is important to discuss who from family members and how they organize active participation in the rehabilitation process according to their free will.

Sometimes what happens with us is unfair, not in time, and "shouldn't be part of our experience, it's not because we are bad or good, it happens. Nobody can predict who is next and what will happen with us in the future. But at the same time, we are not only our trauma; we are much more profound, bigger, and stronger than a traumatic experience. This experience can be integrated into the personality and can support personal growth. Suddenly we can discover the potential which was hidden before and not present.

And life is going on, and always there is a reason. Psychological rehabilitation makes it possible to reliably improve the psychological status of rehabilitants, prevent the development of neurotic reactions to the disease and psychological maladaptation, increase physical rehabilitation indicators, reduce the period of temporary disability and increase the number of people returning to work and social life. And the primary purpose is to improve the quality of life of patients and disabled people.

The problem of stigmatization of disabled people

A number of countries are taking steps to provide disabled people with access to social infrastructure, offer the opportunity to receive education, and regulate their employment. But there is still an attitude toward disabled people, based on stereotypes and low tolerance towards the differences, as a "social burden."

Disability (from the Latin word "invalids" - weak, infirm) is the persistent, long-term, or permanent loss of ability to work, obstacles, or limitations to the activities of a person with physical or mental disabilities. The concept of disability primarily means the loss of a person's ability to work, limiting the fulfillment of their obligations to the state.

There are two main views on the problem of social barriers for disabled people:

1) The social model is based on the fact that society creates difficulties, which does not want to provide equal possibilities for disabled people and people without disability. So the focus is their integration into social processes with equal opportunities, insisting on creating an environment that is accessible to disabled people and adapting the social infrastructure to their needs and requirements;

2) The medical model seems more discriminatory, based on the idea that the reasons for the difficulties of disabled people are in their limited abilities. There is an existing belief that disabled people need assistance in creating a system of specialized institutions for this group of the population, limiting their participation in public life. Most countries of the world are beginning to abandon the medical model.

A more modern model is the social model, which aims to improve the very social status of disabled persons and increase their social activity, giving them the opportunity for self-realization and personal growth. A person with a disability can be an active agent of social space. Society needs to accept it and form an environment that will improve the lives of people with disabilities.

Disability should not be perceived by society as an illness and become a barrier for a person to realize their potential.

This is directly connected with the problem of stigmatization.
Stigmatization is the process of labeling, "stigmatizing" individuals and putting social labels, based on certain externally marked, symbolically expressed characteristics. Putting the pressure and focusing on the differences of this individual compared with all the rest of society, this process limits the abilities of disabled people to take part in social life and events. It can also play a very important role in changes in the person's psychological condition, leading to depressive reactions, suicidal attempts, and progressive isolation. Nicknames, shaming, blaming, and social conflicts are becoming part of those people's painful reality and are increasing the necessity of socio-psychological support.

The cause of stigma is socio-cultural patterns, formalized in social stereotypes and attitudes, and public education on disability issues. The reason for stigma can be any, even the most insignificant natural or social quality, but it is often a negatively perceived trait of character, body, appearance, status. Physical disabilities or health limitations create certain social stereotypes of the surrounding society about their "inferiority" of people with disabilities.

In those severe traumas ок disabilities, psychological aspects of working with stigmatization become an important focus. Working with body changes and limitations, integration, self-acceptance, social image, inner critic, and self-support can significantly influence rehabilitation and improve patients' life quality.

PART 6
WHAT IS SPEECH AND LANGUAGE PATHOLOGY?

Speech and language pathology is a noninvasive, special, interdisciplinary science. Speech-language pathologists evaluate, diagnose, and treat speech, language, communication, and swallowing disorders, regardless of age. These always work as part of a collaborative, interdisciplinary team of professionals, including physical therapists, occupational therapists, social workers, teachers, physicians, audiologists, and psychologists.

Speech and language pathology needs interdisciplinary cooperation in fields:
- *Linguistics:* phonetics, phonology, psycholinguistics, neurolinguistics, sociolinguistics
- *Medicine:* phoniatrics, neurology, neonatology, nutrition, pediatrics, neurosurgery, oncology, plastic surgery, otorhinolaryngology, physiotherapy, psychiatry, radiology
- *Pedagogics:* inclusive pedagogy, special, therapeutic, preschool, and elementary
- *Psychology:* clinical, psychology, clinical neuropsychology, psychotherapy
- *Communication sciences:* informatics, cybernetics, cognitive sciences, media communication

Language differs from speech, which is why speech-language pathology is the study of two fields.

Speech consists of:
- Articulation: How speech sounds are made
- Voice: The use of breathing and vocal cords to produce sounds
- Fluency: The rhythm of speech

Language consists of socially shared rules that include putting words together, making new words, what words mean, and what word combinations are best in what situations.

According to The American Speech-Language-Hearing Association, the following disorders belong to speech-language pathology:

- *Speech Disorders*: Occurs when individuals have difficulty producing speech sounds correctly or fluently
- *Language Disorders*: Occurs when individuals have difficulty understanding others, sharing thoughts, feelings, ideas, and using language in practical and socially appropriate ways. Language disorders may also be in the written form.
- *Social Communication Disorders*: Occurs when individuals have trouble with the social aspect of verbal and nonverbal communication. Individuals with autism spectrum disorders struggle with social communication, as do many individuals with traumatic brain injuries. Those with social communication disorders have difficulty:
  o   Communicating with others socially (greeting others, asking questions.)
  o   Changing their way of communicating depending on the listener or setting
  o   Following socially acceptable rules of conversation and storytelling
- *Cognitive-Communication Disorders*: Occurs when individuals have difficulties paying attention, planning, problem-solving, or organizing their thoughts. These disorders often occur as a result of a traumatic brain injury, stroke, or dementia.
- *Swallowing Disorders:* Occurs when individuals have difficulty in eating and swallowing. Swallowing disorders are often a result of an illness, injury, or stroke.

WHERE CAN YOU FIND SPEECH AND LANGUAGE PATHOLOGISTS?

Speech and language pathologists work in two systems:

1. *Educational system:*
- Centers for special pedagogical and psychological counseling
- Centers of pedagogical-psychological counseling
- Early intervention centers
- Kindergartens
- Primary schools
- Special schools
- Special classrooms at primary schools

2. *Healthcare system:*
- Outpatients departments
- Departments in hospitals and centers:

neurology, psychiatry, otorhinolaryngology, neonatological, NICU, ICU, neurosurgery, long-term ill hospital, geriatrics, pediatrics, plastic surgery, traumatology, phoniatrics, physiotherapy, oncology, dentistry/orthodontics, clinical psychotherapy, spa.

Neonatology Intensive Care Unit (NICU)

The addition of Speech and language pathologists(SLP) to NICU care teams is relatively recent. Their role in the NICU is still developing, but they may be among the first specialists to see a medically stable neonate. A neonate's ability to gain weight in the days and weeks after being born comes down to the ability to feed, and an SLP can be the key to making that happen. Weight gain in neonatal newborns has been shown as a predicting factor in the baby's ability to avoid future complications resulting from premature birth.

Once the SLP has diagnosed any feeding issues, they will work in conjunction with the rest of the care team to develop a treatment plan. This plan may include goals for the infant to improve their food intake, shorten the feeding sessions' length, or increase the baby's comfort as assessed by various visual or behavioral signals offered during the feeding.

It's vital to assess the infant's ability to coordinate the suck-swallow-breathe reflex; a failure to engage motor skills in the correct sequence can lead to aspiration and further breathing complications or even pneumonia.

Oral motor intervention is the primary treatment for issues in this area and can include:

- Non-nutritive sucking
- Oral/perioral stimulation
- Preceding simulation

These interventions have proved effective in reducing the time it takes to transition from nasogastric tubes to regular feeding routines.

They may provide the parents with exercises to perform with the baby or provide them with signs and signals to watch for that could indicate improper physical development and require further intervention.

Dysarthria

Dysarthria is a disorder of motor speech based on organic damage to the nervous system. Respiration, phonation, resonance, articulation are disturbed to varying degrees.

Developmental dysarthria
Developmental dysarthria arises based on a congenital lesion of the nervous system, most often in the context of cerebral palsy syndrome.

Bulbar (hypotonic)
When the motor nuclei of the elongated spinal cord and cranial nerves innervating the speech organs are damaged, sudden accidents, operations in this area arise rather than developmentally.
Mild paralysis with peripheral motoneuron involvement can be unilateral or bilateral.

In the case of bilateral disorder, swallowing and chewing are often impaired and implement articulatory movements.

Spastic (pyramid)
When the central motoneuron failure, part of the spastic form of the Cerebral Palsy.
Speech impaired in the area of targeted respiratory control and velopharyngeal occlusion. It consists of spasmodic, hard, increased nasality, defected rhythm, movements affected by spasticity, cumbersome, and hypertonic with frequent slowly and uncompleted contractions.

Athetoid, hyperkinetic/hypokinetic (extrapyramidal)
In case of failure of the striatum or other subcortical areas in the Cerebral Palsy's dyskinetic form. Articulation indistinct. Some sounds strongly exposed, others weak and indistinct, involuntary movements disrupt chest breathing, formation, and voice stability.

Atactic (cerebellar)
When the brain and its pathways are damaged. Speech is formed explosively, stacca-to-like, emphasis on individual syllables of the word, adiadochokinesis (disability to do quick opposite movements), clumsiness of the tongue, frequent stops in speech, sticking in individual articulatory positions

Mixed
Due to severe lesions or degenerative diseases of the CNS (central nervous system).

Acquired dysarthria
Acquired dysarthria occurs during childhood, adulthood, or aging of an organism, suddenly (brain trauma, infection, CNS cancer) or gradually (degenerative diseases). Dysarthria could be in many neurological syndromes.

Flaccid, peripheral (weak)

When peripheral motoneuron is affected, bulbar paralysis is a part of the neurological syndrome. Present signs of peripheral paresis with atrophy of the affected muscles and small muscle twitches - fasciculations. Monotonous indistinct expression. It is often impaired breathing with hypernasality, hoarseness, and swallowing disorders.

Hypernasality is the most prominent diagnostic feature of flaccid dysarthria. Due to insufficient velopharyngeal occlusion, nasal emissions (leakage of the exhaled air stream through the nose) also occur, and therefore a reduced intraoral pressure is secondary during speech production. These deficits arise mainly in the bilateral lesion of the vagus nerve's pharyngeal branch, which innervates most of the soft palate's muscles.

Articulation disorders occur when the facial nerve (innervating muscles of the lips) and hypoglossus (innervating muscles of the tongue) are damaged, as these nerves are directly involved in the articulation. Bilateral lesions of the facial nerve can significantly affect bilabial (b, p, m) production and labiodental (v, f) consonants.

When the hypoglossal nerve is damaged, it causes the inability to articulate sounds that require the tongue's movement properly. If the lesion hits the trigeminal nerve, which ensures the mandible movement, articulation disorders also occur.

Lack of vocal cord function is caused by incomplete vocal cord closure during phonation (recurrent nerve). Good vocal cord closure is not formed, a voice with a murmur, a whisper.

Present in infectious diseases of the central nervous system, myasthenia gravis, progressive bulbar paralysis, tumors, or stroke in the brainstem area.

Spastic (central)

It's a condition when central motoneuron failure, between the elongated spinal cord and the white matter of the brain's hemispheres. It is part of pseudobulbar paralysis. Present features of central paresis with increased reflexes. Swallowing disorders, restriction, and slowness of movements. Speech slow, laborious, with stretching of words, the incomprehensibility of longer speech. Respiratory weakened and slowed velopharyngeal occlusion, as well as occlusions in articulatory movements.

Muscle spasticity can cause hyperadduction of the vocal cords. A more substantial subglottic pressure is needed to overcome it, and therefore, a phonation with pressure is created.

However, the pathologically increased nasal capacity is milder than in flaccid dysarthria, and there is no noticeable leakage of the exhaled air stream.

Please note that Dysprosody (problems with melody, rhythm, rate, intonation of speech) occurs because spastic muscles have a limited ability to contract and relax. Or - impaired salivation control or less frequent swallowing.

Often in stroke, cerebrovascular diseases, aneurysm rupture, traumatic central nervous system lesion.

Atactic (cerebellar)
It can occur in case of damage to the cerebellum and nerve pathways associated with its activity.

When poorly targeted movements, poor coordination of muscle group activities with general hypotension.

Speech irregular, saccades (explosive words and syllables). Fluctuations in breathing, the intensity of voice, resonance, rhythm, inaccurate realization of especially consonants.

Disorders of articulation of all sounds (consonants and vocals), disorders of prosody (equal emphasis on each syllable, prolonged phonemes, slow speech rate, limited range and intensity of voice), phonation disorders, which manifest as a sharp voice or even a vocal tremor, uncoordinated movements of the respiratory muscles.

In multiple sclerosis, inflammation, and brain tumors, degenerative processes.

Hypokinetic (extrapyramidal)
In the context of the hypokinetic-hypertonic syndrome in disorders of the basal ganglia (Parkinsonism). Rigidity, akinesia of muscle groups, resting routes, and loss of locomotor automatisms. Speech monotonous, initial pause due to muscle stiffness, rapid inaccurate expression with palilalia (repetition of syllables, words), or slows down to stop. Breath is inadequate, intermittent, and voice weakened to aphony.
In Parkinson's disease, sometimes stroke, drug-induced parkinsonism.

Hyperkinetic (extrapyramidal)
Within choreatic or athetoid syndrome, Huntington's disease.

Abnormal involuntary movements, decreased overall muscle tone, increased involuntary muscle movement (speech loud, screaming, discoordination with breathing movements). Speech pace fluctuating, clearly incomprehensible due to inability to control tongue and mouth movements. The cause may be neuroleptics (tardive dyskinesia) or degenerative central nervous system diseases.

Mixed
It occurs in diseases that can affect both the peripheral and central nervous systems.
- Spastic-flaccid dysarthria - amyotrophic lateral sclerosis
- Atactic-spastic dysarthria - multiple sclerosis
- Atactic-spastic and flaccid dysarthria - olivopontocerebellar atrophy
- Spastic-atactic and hypokinetic dysarthria - Wilson's disease
- Hypokinetic-spastic and atactic dysarthria - progressive supranuclear palsy

Anarthria
Practically impossible verbal communication, inability to articulate, loss or non-development of well-controlled movements of articulatory organs. Often associated with aphonia (inability to form a voice)

Diagnostics of dysarthria
Diagnostics of dysarthria is based on a clinical examination of impaired communication skills in terms of form and content, with the main criterion being the intelligibility of speech. The examination of the dysarthria begins with establishing contact with the patient and an initial anamnestic-diagnostic interview. The ability to cooperate, concentration, the ability to exchange communication roles, the level of comprehension of spoken speech, orientation examination of hearing and sight, allo- and autopsychic orientation of the patient and in case of incomprehensible speech or limited cooperation supplement the patient's anamnesis and premorbid level of communication ability from family or acquaintances.

The dysarthria examination itself is focused on:
1. articulatory organs and their motor skills (at rest, their mobility and functionality during movement):
- **lips**: tonus and color, the symmetry of the oral corners, ability to activate during protrusion and retraction, the strength of bilabial closure, possible drooling at rest or when taken orally, pathology in the sense of hyperkinesis of possible lip defects, diadochokinesis

- **tongue**: tone and color, ability to activate without synkinesis of the mandible, lateralization of the tongue at rest and crawling, defects on the tongue, mucosal hydration, pathology in terms of fasciculation, atrophy, diadochokinesis, lateral movements and elevation, the addental position of the apex (tip),
- **dentition**: complete extraction, partial extraction, insufficiency and remediation of teeth, artificial teeth
- **oral cavity:** vein and harsh palate-the strength of the velopharyngeal occlusion at intraoral pressure, the symmetry of the uvula's vein and position at rest and in phonation, possible lateralization of the uvula, gag reflex, will, and reflex cough.
2. **articulation**: isolated sounds according to individual articulation circles and syllables, in a combination of several circles, words, and sentences in conversation, verbal reproduction, reading
3. **phonation**: intensity, height, and quality of voice in spontaneous speech even during targeted tests, phonation time, and phonation method.
4. **respiration**: at rest, in spontaneous speech and phonation, coordination of respiration and phonation and expiration time,
5. **resonance**: the presence of hypo/hypernasality, nasal emissions in spontaneous speech is investigated, and in targeted tests,
6. **prosodic factors:** the pace of speech or bradylalia, intonation (monotonous or bizarre), fluence, dysfunction in the sense of repetitions, iterations or elimination of articles, syllables, or words
7. **deglutination**: the risk of aspiration when eating various consistent foods (solid, liquid, slurry) orally, drooling, inability to swallow one's saliva.

Therapy of dysarthria

Speech and language therapy of dysarthria is noninvasive, symptomatic. It is a behavioral influence on impaired communication skills. This is effective after stabilizing the patient's state of health by a medical and nursing team, which will provide medication, physiotherapy-rehabilitation, surgical or prosthetic therapy according to the patient's needs. As part of clinical speech therapy, preparatory non-specific non-speech procedures are applied, especially at the beginning of the disease in the most severe dysarthria stages, when the orofacial complex's motor is significantly limited.

1. Oromotor exercises aimed at:
- training of the tongue and lips with isotonic and isometric exercises according to the patient's ability actively assisted or passive,
- strengthening the bilabial and velopharyngeal closure,
- training sufficient articulation angle,

- eliminating drooling, hypersalivation, oral and nasal emissions,
- to eliminate synkinesis (involuntary movements) of the intact half of the face, possibly synkinesis of the mandible during tongue movements.
2. **Strengthening or relaxing exercises** of the neck muscles and stabilization of the sciatic and back muscles,
3. **Orofacial point and trajectory stimulation** focused on the toning of the orofacial complex and on the elimination of spasms of the orofacial area,
4. **Respiratory exercises** aimed at the prolongation of oral expiration, deep nasal inspiration, the practice of proper abdominal breathing with diaphragm support, if the patient's condition allows it.
5. **Phonation exercises** aimed at:
- improving the intensity of phonation,
- eliminating micro- or macrophony (low/high voice intensity),
- prolonging the phonation time,
- improving the vocal cord closure,
- eliminating inspiratory phonation,
- soft voice onset in spastic phonation,
- dynamic vocal beginnings in vocal cord hypotension.
6. **Articulation exercises** aimed at practicing intelligible isolated sounds with their fixation and transformation into words and sentences. Subsequent transfer to common verbal communication to move the articulatory base of words as needed forwards or backward at a sufficient articulation angle.
7. **Prosodic exercises** aimed at stabilizing the speech rate by slowing down the tachylalia or accelerating the bradylalia. And eliminating repeats in neurogenic dysfluency, intonation exercises to eliminate monotonicity.
8. Therapy **to eliminate neurogenic dysphagia**
9. Implementation of **augmentative and alternative communication** according to individual mental and physical abilities and possibilities (total immobility) of the patient. Using paper and pencil, whiteboard and erasable marker, mobile phone, iPad, individual picture dictionary, or sounded PC programs with communicators, PC programs controlled by the eye contact, head-mouse.

A significant part of dysarthria therapy is cooperation with relatives, speech therapist's instruction about the patient's communication possibilities, and the applied reeducation methodologies. Patient safety is paramount in both the diagnosis and treatment of dysarthria. Therefore, its correct positioning is critical and ensures team cooperation in the risk of aspiration, silent aspiration in increased congestion.

Developmental dysarthria

In children with central disorders, it is essential to respect the principles of movement development and cooperation with physiotherapy (somatic rehabilitation, induction of a relaxed position with a stable muscle tone of the body, and the use of relaxation). Stimulation should be from the earliest period (stimulation of vital functions of the orofacial tract).

Physiotherapeutic methods used with direct involvement on oromotor system:

Bobath concept

Use of reflex-inhibitory (attenuation) positions and attenuation of unwanted developmentally lower tonic reflexes.

During the Oral therapy to stimulate food intake and swallowing, we provide development of orofacial motor skills (in newborns stimulate missing reflexes (searching, biting, sucking, swallowing, vomiting) active psychomotorics should replace three months of life.

a) **targeted desensitization** in a position that decreases pathological reflexes, stabilizes body tone, reduces body and articulators interactions
b) **articulators massages**
c) **inducing movements** of the articulators using passive movements with assistance, against resistance
d) **food and fluid intake** in a position and manner that does not induce pathological reflexes and stimulates motility
e) **salivation management.**

Speech therapy is using a physiotherapist determined inhibitory position. .

Vojta methodology

The use of spasticity release or attenuation of involuntary movements following exercise. Increase the stimulation of orofacial motor skills and breathing using trigger points in this area during reflex rotation exercises.

Kabat methodology

Exercises against resistance in stimulating the movements of articulation organs.

Orofacial regulatory therapy by Castillo-Morales
Reflex stimulation of the orofacial area's motility, facial muscles, muscles of the thoracic girdle, neck area, and the area of the upper spine. Focuses on the activity of facial muscles, swallowing, and speech. Uses traction, pressure, vibration.

Myofunctional therapy
Elimination of manifestations and consequences of muscle imbalance in the orofacial area by functional stimulation of differentiated motility of parts of articulation organs. Efficiency is mainly in the case of peripheral and functional deviations from the standard.

Speech therapy - core:
- stimulation and fixation of eye contact, tracking the subject
- development of motor imitation, vocalization
- articulators massage connected with meaning sounds
- use semantic sounds as soon as possible to request objects and activities
- create communication exchanges
- stimulation of phonemic hearing
- development of passive vocabulary
- development of spontaneous compensation mechanisms
- breathing, phonation, oromotor and articulation exercises
- rhythmic procedures
- introduction of alternative and augmentative communication (AAK)

Acquired dysarthria
Early start of therapy is required.

Stimulation areas:
- relaxation methods
- respiration
- phonation
- orofacial muscle motility and diadochokinesis
- articulation
- intelligibility and speed of speech
- prosody (sentence intonation, rhythm)
- use of AAK
- use of technical aids (Visible speech, Visible Viewer, PCLX electro-laryngograph, electromyograph, nasometer, Visipitch ...)

Dysarthria type	The dominant area of therapy
Flaccid	Orofacial motoric
	Nasality velopharyngeal occlusion
Spastic	respiration
	articulation
Hyperkinetic	Respiration
	articulation
Hypokinetic	Fonation
	Prosody and resonance
Atactic	Articulation
	prosody

***

Aphasia

Aphasia is an acquired neurogenic communication disorder. It occurs mainly in damage to the left cerebral hemisphere due to:

- vascular brain diseases (hemorrhage, ischemia, hypoperfusion, thrombosis, embolism)
- traumatic lesions of the central nervous system (CNS) (concussion, bruising of the brain)
- CNS cancers
- inflammatory diseases of the brain
- neurodegenerative diseases (Alzheimer, Picka)
- brain intoxication
- children's aphasia

Classification:

Boston

The clinical syndrome of aphasia	Spontaneous speech	Understanding of speech	repeating	naming	reading	writing
Brocka´s aphasia	Nonfluent, agrammatic, paraphasias	Easy to serious difficulties	defective	defective	Often defect	Often defect
Global aphasia	Absence, speech stereotypies	Serious defect	Serious defect	Serious defect	Serious defect (rarely identification of familiar word, name)	Spontaneous scribblements, part of the word
Transcortical motor aphasia	Nonfluent, echolalic	Easy to mild, serious difficulties	Preserved (on the level of words and short sentences)	defective	defective	defective
mixed transkortical aphasia	Nonfluent, speech stereotypies	Seriously defective	preserved, mild defects	Seriously defective	Seriously defective	Seriously defective
Wernicke´s aphasia	Fluent, paraphasias, neologism	Seriously defective	defective	defective	Usually seriously defective	Only high automatic words, paragraphs
Conductive aphasia	fluent	Easy defects	Severe defects, phonemic paraphasias	Easy defects	Quietly relatively well preserved, with loud paralexies	Preserved automatic words
Amnestic, anomic aphasia	Fluent, anomic brakes	Light defects	preserved	defective	Usually preserved	Sometimes semantic paragraphs
Transkortical sensoric aphasia	Fluent, echolalic	Serious defects	preserved, (on the level of words and short sentences) echolalia	defective	Serious defects	Isolated words preserved with understanding serious defects

Lurija´s

Type of aphasia	Primary defect	localization	block	Zone	Central deficit	preserved	defective
dynamic	The planning of speech, defect of inner speech	Frontal lobes	III	Tercial	Defective active speech, the flatness of the psyche	Articulation, reproductive speech, lexia, graphia, occurred perseverations	Low speech activity, initiation, planning, programming, predictivity-use of verbs, a realization of action and its control, productive speech, spontaneous speech, agrammatism, a scheme of sentences, inner speech, mimics, gesticulation, dynamic praxia, spatial orientation, psychics, emotionality, will components
Efferent motor	The sequential organization of movements	precentral	III	Secondary			
Afferent motor	Motor kinesthetic aferentation (transmission of information from the periphery to the center)	postcentral	II	Secondary	Defect of articulation movements, hint doesn´t help	Automatic speech, singing, familiar namesá, emotional manifestation, perseverations, literary paraphasias	Kinesthetic aferentation, feeling of the positioning of the sounds, articulation, secondary understanding of speech, oral praxia, positions of fingers, spatial orientation, graphia, lexia, analyses, synthesis
sensoric	Phonematic hearing	Wernicke´s area temporal	II	Secondary	Defective perception and understanding of speech, failure of the word meaning	Transcription, mimics, gestures, intonation, emotionality, praxia, visual gnosia, space orientation, written calculia, paraphasias neologism, agramatism, logorhoe	phonematic hearing (differentiation), acoustic analysis, perception, understanding, repeating, naming, word structure, logic-grammatical structures, lexia, graphia, singing,acoustic gnosia, loud calculia, feedback, emotionality

Acoustic-mnestic	Acoustic-verbal memory	Middle temporal	II	Secondary	Doesn't understand the hidden text, hint doesn't help	Phonematic hearing, lexia, writing, lost meaning of words, verbal paraphasias	Low verbal-acoustic memory, perception of hidden text, naming, spontaneous speech, repeating, visual gnosia, perception of objects
semantic	Simultan synthesis, spatial operations	Temporalis-parietalis-occipitalis	II	tertial	Defect of understanding of logical-grammatical structures	Expressive speech, lexia, graphia	Logic-grammatical forms, complicated compound sentences, prepositions, stereognosis, constructive praxia, calculia, orientation on the map, clock recognition, comparing constructions, spatial praxia,
amnestic	Defect in choosing alternatives	Back temporal a parietal-occipital area in the dominant hemisphere			A deficit of nominative function, not always a deficiency of mnestic functions	It could be all functions of speech	Naming (global), choosing alternatives,
syndrome occipital lobe		In dominant hemisphere			agnosia visual, of objects, colors, numbers, letters,		
		In nondominant hemisphere			He doesn't recognize people, faces		

Epileptic aphasia in childhood (Landau-Kleffner syndrome)
Sudden start before 7th year and progression, failure of receptive and expressive part of speech. Symptoms are verbal auditive agnosia, the rapid decrease of expression, often behavioral disorders, and difficulties in writing.

Diagnostics of aphasia
The examination of individual functions is preceded by the completion of personal, family, work, and social history, with the acceptance of the primary clinical diagnosis, and a list of other diseases, and the results of ancillary and special examinations. Used an interview maps (indicatively) of the current state, orientation by person, place, time, content, and verbal and nonverbal communication, the concentration of attention, behavior.

Luria's neuropsychological examination **takes 2.5 hours.**
Western Aphasia Battery - WAB (Kertezs, 1982) - 8 subtests (spontaneous speech, comprehension of heard speech, repetition, naming, reading, writing, practice, calculus, construction ability)

Token test
- quantifies speech comprehension and short-term verbal memory

Cognitive -Neuropsychological Model
This is the theory of boxes and arrows.

Boxes have two functions:
1. Reservoir of information
2. Processor of information

Income = recognizing of written and spoken word, direction to the semantic system

Outcome = direction from semantic system to production

Lexicon = vocabulary of known words. There is no information about the pronunciation or meaning of the word

Bumper = its function is like short term memory, then starts neuromuscular programming

Semantic system = data about written and spoken words meaning, use of objects

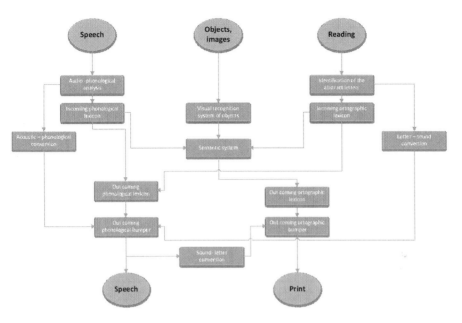

Examination of cortical functions:

- agraphy (spontaneous writing, dictation, copying, drawing)
- speech comprehension (show, give, fulfill, Y / N)
- spontaneous speech (fluency, prosody, paraphasia, paraphrasing, neologisms)
- Gertsman's syndrome (finger agnosis, right-left disorientation, dissociated agraphia, calculia disorder, difficulty understanding the meaning of the words and sentences = parietal lobe lesion)
- alexie (loud reading, silent reading comprehension, identification of graphemes, syllables, words, pseudo text)
- agnosia (optical: objects and colors, prosopagnosia; acoustic, auditory)
- apraxia (structural, motor, ideomotor, ideative)
- somatognosis
- neglect syndrome (neglect of half body and space around)

Diferencial diagnostic aphasia – dementia

	Aphasia	dementia
Start and development of difficulties	Most often acute start and subsequent improvement, residual disability	Most often progressive deterioration with smooth or jumping development of disorders
Social behavior and skills	The predominance of appropriate behavior situations	The predominance of inappropriate behavior situations
Orientation – time, place, person	Intakt, difficulties in expression	The predominance of bad orientation
Short time memory	The predominance of good performance, limited in verbal area	The predominance of bad performance in all componence of memory
Retention of information, skill to learn	Reduced, but saved, possible limit in immediate reaction on stimulus, the better response after delayed reproduction	Overall significantly disturbed, immediate imprinting could be better than delayed reproduction, inability to hold new information in memory
Affects, emotional answers, and personality	Mostly small inconsistent changes	Mostly rising significant changes
Level of insight on difficulties	Lasting and rising insight on difficulties leading to frustration	Gradual or sudden loss of insight and then the absence of frustration
Behavioral and communication activities	It leads to the goal and is intentional	Low or without purpose with shouting, repeating manipulation with objects or cloths
Initiation of activity	Often saved, active initiation of favorite actions	Only rare initiation of any activity
behavior	The predominance of constant, clear, and reasonable behavior	Rising unstable not clear behavior
Communicative behavior	Mostly social adequate with the effort of contact and saved sensitivity to communicational partner, an effort to compensation of speech disorders	Egocentric behavior with failure in conversation, bad eye contact, often the loss of motivation of contact and ability to perceive of needs of a communication partner
Gestural communicational manifestations	Often effort to use gestures and signs, understanding of contents by signs used by communication partner in the effort of understanding	Rare active use, increased restlessness, confusion when others use gestures because they distract from speech
Coherent speech	Predominantly appropriate, limited-expression and perception, in Wernicke´s aphasia, inappropriate speaking	Inappropriate, confused speech, thoughts perseverations, stereotype repeating, development of jargon with perseverations of words and locutions

Therapy of aphasia
Therapeutic directions:

Lurija´s neuropsychological concept renewal of higher mental functions.
Uses involvement of new components, creation of new functional systems (by the renewal of reading letters we use tactile and kinesthetic), inner structurization of activity to lower will control by the defect of will organization, conversion on higher will control (self commenting of own activity) by nondirect methods.

Cognitive-neuropsychological concept
Therapy is concentrated on difficulties in the function of some modality of cognitive processes. It is stimulating and facilitating technics to use transfer, where reduction of concrete cognitive modality problems shows improvement in communication.

Melodic-intonational therapy (MIT)
Effective in people with preserved ability to reproduce melody.

Reduction of perseverations
It helps to get conscious control of the start of self speech production. Make a more extended break between showing stimuli and his naming, using another modality (gestures, the first letter of the word, drawing), ending sentences.

Phonemic-visual stimulation
By severe aphasia and oral dyspraxia. Development of oral praxia with graphic and phonemic contents. Using graphical phonemic images for a stable auditive reaction. Using isolated vowels in rhythmic or melodic-intonational structures of words and sentences. Support of repeating of the global word and sentence lines and involve them into speech.

PACE- Promoting Aphasics Communicative Effectiveness
For better effectivity of communication by role play of common situation of changing information , free choose of modality.

Conversational analysis and conversational stimulation skills (conversational coaching)
They are using compensational communication strategies in producing information. Patient with therapist create scenario of 6-8 sentences, they train it many times, and the patient uses this with a family member. The process is videotaped.

Using nonverbal ways of communication
Primarily by global aphasia. Using pictograms, conceptual drawings, gestures, signs, drawings. Visual Action Therapy.

Therapy in groups
For facilitation of conversation, maximalization communication effectiveness. The therapist is a facilitator.

Developmental verbal dyspraxia

Developmental verbal dyspraxia (childhood apraxia of speech, developmental apraxia of speech) is a neurological developmental disorder of the speech's sound plane. The accuracy and consistency of movements during articulation are impaired.

The disruption is at the deep processes level, with no neuromuscular deficits (such as abnormal reflexes, abnormal tone). It can occur as a result of a known neurological disorder or in combination with neurobehavioral disorders (genetic, metabolic) of known or unknown origin or as an idiopathic (without neurological or neurobehavioral disorders) neurogenic disorder of the sound plane of speech.

A fundamental deficit is considered a disruption of the planning and/or programming of Spatio-temporal parameters of speech motor sequences, which disrupts speech production and prosody.

It is a disorder of the ability to perform learned movements, a disorder of motor planning. It differs from dysarthria in that there is no paresis, weakness, or impaired muscle coordination. When examining automatic and reflex movements (smile, cough, etc.), muscle function is normal.

Terminology problems:

Developmental oral dyspraxia The inability or difficulty to have will control non-speech movements (such as blowing, swollen lips). These same movements are intact at the reflex level. The client can perform them spontaneously, but not on request.

Developmental articulatory dyspraxia disturbance of movements in the formation of individual sounds. He has a problem uttering isolated articulatory demanding sounds. Articulatory deficits as part of the disorder. There are also mild degrees of developmental verbal dyspraxia when dyspraxia is diagnosed at the age of eight.

It is questionable how to distinguish developmental articulatory dyspraxia from articulatory disorder.

Developmental verbal dyspraxia, according to Dvořák (1999), is a specific developmental deviation of speech expression at the word level. The problem with realizing the word occurs regardless of whether or not the child can physiologically manage the sound's articulation. Longer words are articulated worse, and faster speech causes a worse articulatory performance

Ten features typical for the diagnosis of developmental verbal dyspraxia:
1. Impaired articulation of vowels in terms of vocal distortion.
2. Difficulties in taking initial articulatory configurations or in transitioning from one articulatory position to another.
3. The problem of adequately expressing emphasis in a word or sentence.
4. Syllable segregation, interrupting the smooth transition between syllables in or between words. This causes the articulation to be interrupted for a few milliseconds (staccato).
5. Groping or prolongations - the child tries to practice, adjust the articulatory position needed to produce sounds or combine sounds.
6. Disturbing indefinite "schwa" vowels (insert an unclear sound into the word, especially between two consonants).
7. Errors in soundless sounds (exchange of voiced and unvoiced sounds, loss of sound).
8. Slow speech rate at the level of syllables, words, and sentences (as a compensatory strategy). The child purposefully slows down the speech rate so that he can hear his pronunciation by listening.
9. Distortions and substitutions of consonants.
10. Difficulties in articulation are more pronounced in multi-syllable words (the number of articulation errors increases unnaturally)

Three significant features differentiate developmental verbal dyspraxia/childhood apraxia of speech from other childhood speech sound disorders. These features are:

- Inconsistent errors on consonants and vowels in repeated productions of syllables and words
- Lengthened coarticuclatory transitions between sounds and syllables
- Inappropriate prosody, especially in the realization of lexical or phrasal stress

Diagnostics of developmental verbal dyspraxia

Developmental verbal dyspraxia can be diagnosed through specific exams that measure oral speech mechanisms (pursing lips, blowing, licking lips, elevating the tongue, an examination of the mouth). A complete exam also involves observation of the patient eating and talking.

Apraxia experts warn against giving an official diagnosis until a child is roughly three years old when other speech delays have been ruled out. Risks are:
- Limited/no babbling
- Loss of words previously used
- Says a word differently with each try
- Lack of phonetic diversity
- Inconsistent errors
- Feeding difficulties
- Limited intonation

Need to be observed:
1. Phonetic repertoire, including vocals and diphthongs, used by the child in the spontaneous one-word naming of images.
2. The phonetic repertoire that the child uses during spontaneous production in a multi-sentence conversation.
3. Level of phonotactic development (how many syllable words he uses).
4. Whether the child has a reduced phonetic repertoire compared to peers.
5. Whether the performances in the production of vowels in one-word spontaneous output are better than the performances in the production of vowels in a multi-sentence spontaneous speech
6. Phonological processes with a focus on monitoring the loss of annoyance, metathesis, and the elimination of consonants
7. Consistency of speech. The consistency test consists of naming 25 images in three experiments. Subsequently, the percentage of inconsistently spoken words is calculated. If the inconsistency is more than 40%, it is considered a pathological condition.
8. Sound level of speech during imitation. Repetition of words. Whether the production of a child's phonetic repertoire is worse in conscious repetition of words than spontaneous production.

Syllable Repetition Test (SRT) **determines if a child will make planning and programming errors while repeating** longer meaningless audio units.

Repetition - prolonging words and sentences to determine whether the differences in production are caused by changing the length of the word and sentence. With the increasing linguistic structure, the number of speech production errors in children with developmental verbal dyspraxia increases.

During the diagnosis of verbal production, both spontaneous and imitated, we observe the presence of prolongations, "schwa" sound, syllabic segregation, resonance, nasality, speech rate, groping, adjustment of articulatory organs, the omission of consonants, confusion of consonants, confusion of annoyance and problems. with vocals

9. Diadochokinesis (the ability to perform alternating rapidly opposite movements). Examine motor control during speech production
10. Oromotor abilities, if a child has problems with non-speech isolated or sequential oromotor movements.
11. Prosody, if the child can imitate the melody and sentence emphasis.
12. Phonation (respiratory and laryngeal capacity and voice quality).
13. Orientation examination of dynamic practice, imitation learning in tasks that require motor planning and motor coordination of movements
14. Examination of the oral phases of eating and drinking, focusing on the mobility of the lips, tongue, bite, chewing, and swallowing.
15. Indicative assessment of the child's language skills

Therapy of developmental verbal dyspraxia
American Speech-language-hearing Association divides treatment options of developmental verbal dyspraxia into four categories:

1. Motor-Programming
2. Linguistic
3. Sensory Cueing
4. Rhythmic
5. Combination (usually a motor-programming approach combined with one of the above)
6. Augmentative and Alternative Communication (sign language, tablet with communication apps, speech-generating device, communication book).

Sometimes parents or caregivers are worried that these technologies will stunt language learning, but this isn't the case. Augmentative and Alternative Communication is usually used in the early stages of intervention, and as the individual's speech grows, they typically self-select speech over AAC. At times some individuals with severe apraxia may need to continue using AAC methods.

Integral stimulation is based on cognitive-motor learning, focusing on the cognitive-motor planning needed for the complex motor task of speech, "watch me, listen, do as I do" It uses various modalities of presentation, emphasizing the auditory and visual modes.

The integrated phonological approach incorporates targeted speech production practice into phonological awareness activities and uses letters and phonological cues to prompt speech production.

Acquired apraxia of speech

It is a neurogenic communication disorder affecting speech production's motor programming system—difficulty in speech production, specifically sequencing and forming sounds. The Levelt model describes the speech production process in the following three consecutive stages: conceptualization, formulation, and articulation. According to the Levelt model, apraxia of speech would fall into the articulation region. The individual does not suffer from a language deficiency but has difficulty in producing language audibly. Notably, this difficulty is limited to vocal speech and does not affect sign-language production. The individual knows exactly what they want to say, but a disruption in the brain sends the signal to the specific movement's muscle.

Wertz et al. (1984) describe the following five speech characteristics that an individual with apraxia of speech may exhibit:

- **Effortful trial and error with groping**
  - Groping is when the mouth searches for the position needed to create a sound. When this trial and error process occurs, sounds may be held out longer, repeated, or silently voiced. May be able to produce certain sounds independently, quickly, and unconsciously. However, when prompted by another to create the same sound, the patient may grope with their lips, using volitional control (conscious awareness of the attempted speech movements), struggling to make the sound.

  -**Self-correction of errors**
  - Patients are aware of their speech errors and can attempt to correct themselves. This can involve distorted consonants, vowels, and sound substitutions.

- **Abnormal rhythm, stress, and intonation**
- Include irregular pitch, rate, and rhythm. Speech can be too slow or too fast and highly segmented (many pauses), monotone, 'robotic'.

- **Inconsistent articulation errors on repeated speech productions of the same utterance**
- When producing the same utterance in different instances, it may be difficult to use and maintain the same articulation that was previously used for that utterance. Articulation also becomes more complicated when a word or phrase requires an articulation adjustment, in which the lips and tongue must move to shift between sounds.

- **Difficulty initiating utterances**
- Errors in completing a speech movement gesture may increase as the length of the utterance increases. Targeted use of simple syllables and a limited range of consonants and vowels.

Therapy of Acquired Apraxia of speech

There are four main categories of treatment:

1. *Articulatory-kinematic treatments* - to improve speech (modeling or repetition) and improve speech production's spatial and temporal aspects.
2. *Rate and rhythm control treatments* - to improve errors in patients' timing of speech (an external source of control like metronomic pacing)
3. *Intersystemic reorganization/facilitation techniques.* Gestures are usually combined with verbalization. It is thought that it may improve the organization of speech production.
4. *Alternative and augmentative communication approaches* are highly individualized for each patient. However, they often involve a "comprehensive communication system" that may include "speech, a communication book aid, a spelling system, a drawing system, a gestural system, technologies, and informed speech partners."

PROMT is a specific treatment method (Prompts for Restructuring Oral Muscular Phonetic Targets), integrates physical-sensory, cognitive-linguistic, and social-emotional aspects of motor performance. The main focus is developing language interaction through this tactile-kinetic approach by using touch cues to facilitate the articulatory movements associated with individual phonemes, and eventually, words.

One study describes the use of *electropalatography* (EPG) to treat a patient with severe acquired apraxia of speech. The program allows patients to see articulators' placement during speech production, thus helping them correct errors.

Stuttering

It is a syndrome of complex disruption of organ coordination participating on speaking. Primarily manifested with involuntary (tonic, clonic) disrupting of the speaking process fluency. Primarily it is a disruption of nonsymbolic processes, but secondary, this affects symbolic processes also.

There are three areas of symptoms – dysfluency, effort, tension.

Types of dysfluencies:

1. repetitions
parts of words: ba - ba - ba - basketball
whole words: How old are are are you?
word phrases: I was I was I was at home

2. prolongations
vowels/syllables: lllllllllletś go home

3. silent prolongations: try with a big effort to say a word, and he is silent

4. disconnected words
there was so woder- (pause)-full

5. interjections
vowels/syllables: um...um I have problem
whole words: I have yes this problem
word phrases: I have you know the problem

6. silent pauses: I was (obvious and incorrect placed pause) in the shop
7. incomplete word phrases: I don´t know if I could... lt´s go home
8. reparations: I think I will go home, for a walk

Abnormal effort:
1. stop
2. impaired coverbal behavior

3. irregular acceleration of pace in dysfluency
4. starters
5. vegetative symptoms

Psychical tension:
1. avoidant behavior
2. ticks
3. absence of eye contact
4. manipulation with clothes, objects, body
5. tremor of hands
6. logophobia, anxiety

Hysterical stuttering – developed from another severe clinical problem with psychopatic features. There are no tonuses, and clones usually occur repeating syllables, words, and whole phrases.

Aphasic stuttering – developed on the brain damage.

Traumatic stuttering – often after severe psychotrauma, prolonged mutism, a vocal extension on the beginning or end of the words, embolophonias during speaking, a sudden occurrence of symptomatic with immediate fixation.

Cluttering

It is a disorder of speech fluency with excessive speaking speed, and it´s an irregularity, intraverbal and interverbal accelerations, significant fluctuation of rate, interrupted fluency, manifestations of stuttering, difficulties in the articulation of long words with consonants clusters, deficits in narrative and pragmatic skills, deficits in concentration, hyperactivity, specific learning difficulties,

Variable symptoms:
- small vocabulary (do not use prepositions, confused)
- poor syntactic structures (sentence formation)
- incorrect grammar
- constant errors
- one does not "manage" to articulate all the sounds correctly
- contamination (shuffling, mixing syllables or sounds)
- elice (omission)
- dysfluency (repetition, prolongation)

- symptoms worsen with relaxation, improve with concentration
- intraword and interword accelerations
- the longer the speech section, the greater the chance of acceleration
- irregularity of speech rate (and overall speech)
- breathing problem (acceleration disrupts the breathing process)
- deteriorated level of language expressions
- indistinct articulation
- pathologically accelerated pace of speech

Diagnostics of Stuttering

Diagnostic could be realized on three hierarchic organized levels. Orientational (Is there some kind of impaired communication ability?), primary (What kind of impaired communication ability?), specific (What type, form, a degree is it?).
Lechta (2005) made an algorithm of complex diagnostic:

Material	Use/component of diagnostic
An audiotape of spontaneous speaking (conversation at home)	Basic information
Video/audiotape of guided interview	Degree of impairment (respiration, phonation, articulation, prosody, effort, tension) Transcription (type and localization of dysfluencies, effort, tension) Quantification (quantity and percentage of dysfluencies)
Tasks of balbutiogram (whispering, simultaneous speech, singing, automatic speaking, repeating, finishing sentences, reading, spontaneous speech)	Balbutiogram Index of adaptation Index of consistence
Control evaluation (video/audiotape of guided interview)	Index of improvement/deterioration Degree of impairment

Riley´s scale **is used for the evaluation of separated symptoms.**
0 doesn´t occur
1. is not perceptible if we don´t look for it
2. perceptible to the random listener
3. makes the listener uncertain
4. very distracting
5. persistent and severe

Frequence of stuttering per minute

Randall-Jehle coefficient of stuttering: $\dfrac{\Sigma \text{ of all dysfluencies} \times 100}{\Sigma \text{ of all words}}$

Index of consistence: $\dfrac{\Sigma \text{ symptoms located on the same place repeatedly} \times 100}{\Sigma \text{ all symptoms}}$

Index of adaptation: $\dfrac{\Sigma \text{ dysfluencies at first reading (speaking)}}{\Sigma \text{ dysfluencies at repeating reading (speaking) of the same text}}$

Index of improvement/ deterioration: $\dfrac{\Sigma \text{ dysfluencies by controled evaluation}}{\Sigma \text{ dysfluencies at first evaluation}}$

Diagnostics of Cluttering

- Known are Predictive Cluttering Inventory – analysis of spontaneous speech, reading and storytelling, phonological and oral-motor skills.
- It is crucial to evaluate mental development, language skills, the correlation between cognitive and language development, and then the occurrence of dysfluency speech, semantic, syntactic, and phonetic structure of speech, the pace of speech.
- Helpful are EEG and EMG results.

Differential diagnoses:

	Balbuties	Tumultus sermonis
Adaptation effect	yes	No
Logophobia (fear of speaking)	Often progress	No
Awareness about deficit	yes	No
Specific symptoms	Prolongations, repeating, spasms	Repeating, without spasms
Concentration on speaking	Negative effect	Positive effect
Relaxation	Positive effect	Negative effect
Fear of certain sounds	yes	No
Reading familiar text	improvement	Without improvement
Lee´s effect (delaeyed own audiofeedback)	weakening	deterioration
psychics	shyness	careless

Therapy of Stuttering

Therapy of stuttering needs an interdisciplinary approach (speech and language pathologist, physician, psychologist).

Syndrome of stuttering is about the mutual blending of three symptom groups: dysfluency, effort, tension.

Incipient stuttering
- **Tension** – preventive therapy
- **Effort** – behavioral technics (systematical desensibilisation), children's yoga
- **Dysfluency** – phonographorythmic (creating of fluency)
- *Fixated stuttering (6.-13.year)*

Using PROLAM GM (operational conditioning, transfer, and fixation)
- **Tension** – change of attitude, self-monitoring
- **Effort** – physiological improvement, manipulation of length and complexity of speech changing
- **Dysfluency** – manipulation of speech fluency

Chronic stuttering
- **Using MID** by Van Riper (modification of tension and effort by changing of attitude)
- **Tension** – psychotherapy
- **Effort** – systematical desensibilisation, autogenous training
- **Dysfluency** – VAS from therapy by Van Riper (modification of dysfluency, change of anxiety/logophobia), treatment by Ronald Webster (fluency shaping)

Indirect approach	Direct approach
Aimed at surroundings influential, the personality of a stutterer, or in general his language, motor ability, without direct training of fluency.	Explicit, open, and direct influence on verbal expression and related behavior. Reduction of anxiety.
Direct stutterer handling	*Fluency shaping*
Communication ability, speech, and language development stimulation, yoga, relaxation, therapy with play, logarithmic, music therapy,	Fluent items before therapy expand by using operational conditioning: rhythmic speech, reduced pace of speech, voice onset change, using technics (delayed auditive feedback, white noise, metronome)
Change of attitudes and feelings, get the realistic attitude to stuttering	Transfer to everyday communication situations
Concentration improvement, an extension of auditory processing capacity, oromotor coordination improvement	stabilization
Indirect stutterer handling	*Stuttering modification*

Guidance	Changing of speaking pattern, improvement of motor coordination (respiration, phonation, articulation)
Cognitive stuttering processing	Correction of certain symptoms, gradual modification of symptoms after Van Riper, correction of coverbal behavior
Emotional-affective stuttering processing	
Behavioral processing	

Therapy of Cluttering

The main problem is that the person is unaware of the problem. Tarkowski (2002) says that it´s essential to concentrate on:

- *The motivation* for attending therapy
- *Organization* of speaking structure. Technics of verbal thinking (De Bono, 1995), rhetorics technics, training of interpersonal communication
- *Stabilization* of results.

Methods:
- Modification of the speech speed. Using Delayed auditory feedback.
- Development of awareness of fluency or dysfluency of own speech,
- Development of lexical, semantic, and pragmatic skills, speech coherrention (cohesion)
- Using audio and video records,
- Relaxation and imagination therapy
- Positive self talk
- Cognitive training

Dysphagia

The swallowing process requires proper coordination of the oral cavity function, pharynx, larynx, and esophagus. The physiological processes of chewing and swallowing require the integration of the movements of the mimic and masticatory muscles, the muscles of the tongue, the soft palate, and the pharynx muscles in coordination with the activity of the laryngeal muscles and the control of respiration.

Swallowing is a complex and well-coordinated process that requires precise interaction between several areas of the central nervous system, sensory and motor nerves, and peripheral receptors of pressure, temperature, chemical stimuli, and water.

Swallowing in children and adults is different, not only due to various anatomical conditions. In the pediatric population, the ongoing development of the organs involved in swallowing also plays a role.

Therefore, the classification, diagnosis, and treatment also differ in part.

Dysphagia, in general, can be divided from several points of view:
- *In terms of ontogenesis:* congenital, acquired
- *In terms of control and execution of the swallowing process:* neurogenic, structural, mixed
- *In terms of morphological integrity of organs:* anatomically conditioned, functional
- *In terms of time:* acute, chronic
- *In terms of localization:* oropharyngeal (preesophageal), esophageal (esophageal), postesophageal (esophagogastric), paraesophageal (extrinsic dysphagia)
- *In terms of the etiology of origin:* inflammatory, traumatic, iatrogenic, congenital, autoimmune, metabolic, others.

Childhood dysphagia
- swallow disorders, which are disorders of the swallowing phases
- and/or behavioral and sensory feeding problems, where the swallowing stages are not disturbed, but the child has not undergone stages of developing the acquisition of oral motor skills and abilities due to long-term nonoral food intake or due to remaining at a certain stage of food intake (does not go to the stage of biting, chewing of solid consistency, rejects a certain consistency, accepts only a particular type of diet.

Causes of childhood dysphagia:
- Neurological diseases (DMO, brain trauma, meningitis)
- Congenital cardiovascular diseases (congenital heart disease,
- Respiratory diseases (chronic obstructive pulmonary disease)
- Genetic syndromes (Down's, Charge's)
- Sensory problems (hypo and hypersensitivity in the oral cavity)
- Gastrointestinal diseases (atresia, esophageal stenosis, GER)
- Premature birth, low birth weight
- Socio-emotional causes (anxiety, mother-child disorder)

Symptoms of childhood dysphagia
Newborn and baby

Direct warning signals:
- Absence of oral reflexes
- Impaired coordination of respiration, suction, and swallowing
- Weak, uncoordinated suction
- Delay of swallowing reflex
- Vomiting during a meal or after eating
- Nasal penetration during sucking
- Cough while eating

Indirect warning signals:
- Apnoeic pauses
- Heart rate slowing
- Respiratory rate acceleration
- Refusal to eat
- Long feeding time, the baby is dissatisfied during it
- Intermittent sucking with frequent breaths
- Mucus obstruction
- Changes in the color of the skin blue or tears

Toddlers and older children:

Direct warning signals:
- Delayed or abnormal, pathological, a disturbed development of oromotor system movements
- Impaired oromotor and sensorimotor abilities (immature biting and chewing, imperfect bolus shift)
- During feeding and swallowing, the baby has an unusual head and neck position (incorrect posture)
- Voice changes after swallowing
- Weakened voluntary cough
- Cough or suffocation during or after a meal
- Reflux
- Unexplained weight loss
- Significantly shortened language bridle
- Losing food from the mouth

- Hypersalivation
- Uneven, disturbed, abnormal muscle tone

Indirect warning signals:
- Anorexia
- Stomach ache
- Frequent respiratory infections
- Chest pain
- Smelly breath
- Abnormal behavior during meals
- Eating time more than 30 minutes
- Imperfect, immature fencing and chewing
- Imperfect bolus shift
- Slow eating
- Feeling of food sticking in your throat or discomfort when swallowed
- Loss of appetite
- Rejection of a certain consistency of food

Dysphagia in adults
- *Causes of dysphagia in adults:*
- Neurological and degenerative diseases: stroke, tumors, brain injuries, ALS, SM, Alzheimer, Parkinson, dementia, muscular dystrophy, myasthenia gravis, Huntington chorea, dystonia, bulbar paralysis, neuro infection)
- Congenital diseases (developmental anomalies, clefts, tracheoesophageal fistulas)
- Inflammatory systemic diseases (polymyositis, rheumatoid arthritic scleroderma)
- Viral diseases (Guillain-Barré syndrome...)
- After surgery (tracheostomy, surgery in oral cavity, pharynx, larynx, thyroid, spine, cranial base).
- Esophageal reflux (hoarseness, frequent coughing, feeling full throat, chronic cough)
- Oncological diseases in the area of the oral cavity, larynx, and pharynx (postoperative and radiological consequences)
- Traumas in the orofacial and laryngopharyngeal area (perforation injuries, foreign body in the oropharynx, esophagus)
- Cervical spine diseases (cervical osteophytes, changes in the jaw joint)
- Geriatric syndrome (physiological changes after 65 years, reduction of saliva secretion, deterioration of organ coordination, reduction of sensitivity in the area of larynx and pharynx, destruction of pharyngeal smooth muscles, and the slowdown of esophageal peristaltic)

- Psychogenic dysphagia (most common sign is the fear of swallowing)

Symptoms of dysphagia in adults

The highly complex physiological course of swallowing works typically without difficulty. However, dysfunction of even one of the organs involved in swallowing disrupts the swallowing process. Failure of one phase of swallowing will also negatively affect the other stages of swallowing.

Symptoms of dysphagia in adults due to impaired oral or pharyngeal swallowing are:
- Leaking: penetration of a bite of varying consistency from the nose
- Drooling: loss of a bite of varying consistency from the mouth, impaired sensitivity in the oral cavity
- Leftovers in the mouth after swallowing
- Feeling of a foreign body in the "throat."
- Moist or bubbly voice during or after swallowing
- Cough during or immediately after swallowing
- Problems with breathing and swallowing coordination
- Frequent aspiration pneumonia / respiratory infection and fever
- Extra effort or time required for chewing or swallowing
- Changes in eating habits, avoiding certain foods/drinks
- Weight loss or dehydration due to lack of diet

Diagnostics of dysphagia

Diagnosis and treatment of adult and pediatric patients with dysphagia is part of the procedure of a multidisciplinary dysphagiological team, which consists of experts in medical and non-medical disciplines.

The occurrence of swallowing disorders in the family, the occurrence of diseases in the family that could cause dysphagia in the child, the current way of eating (oral, nonoral), neonates and in infants, also the posture of the body during feeding, the timing of feeding the child, intervals between individual stages of feeding, in toddlers and the elderly, independence in eating and nutritional status.

- Processing medical documentation (health status of the child, the course of pregnancy, childbirth, postpartum adaptation, etc.)
- Orientational observation of the child evaluate:
  o the degree of development of gross motor skills of the child, as well as the posture and symmetry of the body

o the degree of development of fine motor skills and the presence of individual grips
- Palpation examination of orofacial structures with sensitivity and motor skills (oral reflexes, movements of the jaw, lips, tongue, appearance of the hard and soft palate and oral mucosa)
- Evaluation of the child's reactions to tactile, acoustic, and visual stimuli
- Indicative assessment of the child's language system
- Indicative assessment of the child's respiration, nasality, and phonation
- Observation of the child at feeding, during food intake (the body's position during eating, the method of food intake, consistency, structure and volume of food, and behavior of the child during eating, in neonates and infants, non-nutritive sucking, changes in breathing during feeding, baby's skin color)
- Evaluation of diagnostic results, the decision on next steps
- Counseling for parents: an acquaintance of parents with the child's clinical picture and its prognosis, with the proposed treatment plan, approach the instrumental examination.

INSTRUMENT EXAMINATION

1. **VideoFluoroscopic Swallow Study (VFSS)** is a radiological examination. It is usually performed by a doctor-radiologist and a clinical speech and language pathologist. Three consistencies are given: liquid, slurry, and solid. It is recommended to first administer fluid (1-2 swallows), in a volume of 2-3 ml, which corresponds to the saliva volume in one typical swallow.

At the first detection of aspiration, find out whether the child aspires to other consistencies of different viscosity and temperature. If there is no significant aspiration, continuous drinking from a bottle or cup (depending on the child's age) is monitored to assess the child's oromotor skills, nutritional sucking rhythm, oral swallowing phase parameters, and elimination of penetration (mouthpiece into the larynx) or aspiration.

If fluid aspiration occurs, the safety of receiving additional consistency should be tested. It is continued by eating a slurry with a spoon, and a solid consistency to assess other oromotor skills, initiate the swallowing reflex, eliminate residues in the oropharyngeal swallowing phase, and evaluate the size and duration of upper esophageal sphincter opening.

2. **Flexible Endoscopic Evaluation of Swallowing (FEES)** is performed by an EarNoseThroat doctor and a clinical speech and language pathologist. Even with

FEES, three consistencies are usually given: liquid, slurry, and solid. In addition to the above examinations, other examination methods can be used in the diagnosis of swallowing disorders, such as transnasal esophagoscopy, CT, MRI, esophageal pH-meter, esophageal manometry.

Diagnostic in adults

In case of positive screening for swallowing and suspicion of dysphagia and/or aspiration, basic clinical-speech therapy, suspicion of dysphagia and aspiration, and an instrumental examination of swallowing.

BASIC CLINICAL EXAMINATION

1. It is obtaining an objective (from family members, medical staff) and subjective (from the patient) anamnesis. It focuses on eating difficulty, difficulty swallowing, coughing when drinking fluids, suffocation during meals, etc.
2. Processing of medical documentation: medical findings related to the location of the brain lesion, bronchopulmonary complications, operations in the oral cavity, larynx, pharynx. We find data on aphasia, dysarthria, abnormal cough, voice changes after swallowing, weight loss, and saliva. In the form of an interview, we will also determine the degree of consciousness, the level of cognitive abilities, and the patient's motivational abilities (e.g. questions focused on how the patient received food so far, whether he had a tracheostomy, whether he was intubated, etc.)
3. Structural and functional examinations of the organs involved in swallowing, including examination of the cranial nerves
4. Evaluation of the patient's current ability to swallow using "water tests" (to detect aspiration) and evaluation of swallowing of other consistencies. Daniels test, GUSS (Gugging Swallowing Screen) screening test.
5. Evaluation of diagnostic results, the decision on next steps
6. Counseling for the patient and his family members

INSTRUMENT EXAMINATION

As in pediatric dysphagia, FEES and VFSS methods are used to diagnose dysphagia in adults and are considered the "gold standard."

Penetration-aspiration scale

Degree	Localization of food in the respiratory tract	evaluation
1.	It does not enter the respiratory system	Norm
2	It enters the respiratory organs, does not reach the level of the vocal cords. It is completely expelled	penetration
3.	It enters the respiratory organs, does not reach the level of the vocal cords, it is not expelled	Penetration
4	It enters the respiratory organs, reaches the level of the vocal cords, and is expelled	Penetration
5.	It enters the respiratory organs, reaches the level of the vocal cords, is not expelled	Penetration
6.	It enters the respiratory system gets below the level of the vocal cords; it is expelled	Aspiration
7.	He gets below the vocal cord level; despite his efforts, he is not expelled	Aspiration
8.	He gets below the vocal cord level without any effort to expel it	aspiration

Daniels test

2x 5ml, 2x10ml, 2x20ml water drink. The test is positive for aspiration if at least 2 of the six symptoms are present:

- dysarthria (impairment of muscular control, respiration, articulation, phonation, resonance and/or prosody)
- dysphonia (impairment of quality, pitch, strength, voice)
- abnormal will cough (weak, unvoiced, absent)
- abnormal or missing gag reflex (missing or weakened contraction of the soft climate or posterior pharyngeal wall, before the test)
- cough swallow (immediately or within 1 minute)

GUSS Gugging Swallowing screen.

Indirect test

		yes	No
Vigilance: the patient must be awake for at least 15 minutes		1	0
Cough and/or coughing	Will cough The patient should cough or cough twice	1	0
Swallowing saliva:			

Swallowing successful		1	0
Drooling		0	1
Change of voice (hoarse, bubbling, damp, veiled, weak voice		0	1
	completely	(5) 1-4= stop the investigation and continue later 5= continue with part 2	

Direct swallow test

Order	1	2	3
	concentrated liquid	liquid	Solid food
Swallowing:			
Swallowing is not possible	0	0	0
Delayed swallowing (>2sek.)	1	1	1
Solid consistence>10sek.	1	1	1
Successful swallowing	2	2	2
cough: (reflexive, before, during, or after swallow with delay to 3 min.)			
Yes	0	0	0
No	1	1	1
drooling:			
Yes	0	0	0
No	1	1	1
Change of voice: (before and after swallow when saying „O")			
Yes	0	0	0
No	1	1	1
comletely	(5)	(5)	(5)
	1-4= stop the investigation and continue later	1-4= stop the investigation and continue later	1-4= stop the investigation and continue later
	5=continue with liquids	5=continue with solid food	5=norm
Total (sum of indirect and direct swallow test results			20

Dysphagia:
1. Oropharyngeal – problem befor and during swallowing
2. Esophageal – problem after swallowing:
   a) mechanical barrier – problem with solid food
   b) defect of motility of esophagus – problem with solid and liquid food

Therapy of dysphagia

Therapy in children

The primary goal is to work with physicians to provide adequate nutrition and hydration that is safe for the child without aspiration. Orofacial stimulation is often used by various techniques, using Premature Infant Oral Motor Intervention (PIOMI), Morales orofacial regulation therapy (ORT), or using thermotactic stimulation non-nutritive suction training. Speech therapist stimulates all functions that are important for adequate psychomotor and social development of the child and the development of speech and language.

Art –developed general principles for feeding children of all ages:

- Regular mode, in a quiet environment, without distractions, without games, food not as a reward
- Eating is limited to about 30 minutes.
- The child should be comfortable and concerned about his motor development if he cannot sit independently and in a "suitable" seat.
- The child should be supported as much as possible in independent eating.
- Take food from a child if he started playing with food without eating or throws it in anger.

Therapy in adults

There are direct and indirect forms of treatment in adult patients with dysphagia.

1.Indirect treatment

Swallowing training without food. It aims to improve the strength and coordination of the muscles involved in the oral and pharyngeal phases of swallowing. This form of treatment is used in patients in whom it is not possible to induce the pharyngeal swallow phase or who are fed via NasoGastricSonde (NSG) or Percutaneous Endoscopic Gastrostomy (PEG) due to the significant aspiration of all food consistencies.

This includes thermo-tactile stimulation, Masako maneuver, etc. In recent years, electrostimulation using electrodes placed on the skin has also become very active.

Training of oral phase:

Maneuver/exercise	goal	Indirect therapy	Direct therapy
Swallow with effort	Strengthens tongue radix and strength of pharynx, increases pressure	yes	yes
Therapy with gauze	Improves oral control of bolus and strength of chewing	yes	No
Tongue resistance	Strengthens the tongue	yes	No
Mendelson´s maneuver	Strengthens elevation of the tongue, the prolonged opening of upper esophagus closure	yes	yes
Super-supraglottic swallow	Improves tongue strength, helps to close larynx closure before and during a swallow	yes	Yes
Supraglottic swallow	Protects respiratory system before the swallow	yes	Yes
Strengthens of the pharynx	Improves movements anteroposterior of pharynx closures	yes	No
Termotactile stimulation	Improves initiation of the pharyngeal phase	yes	yes
Training of vocal cords adduction	Improves vocal cord closure	yes	No

Training of pharyngeal phase:
- **Pharynx strengthens** – tongue hold maneuver
- **Radix tongue strengthens** – swallow with effort
- **Strengthens of the vocal cord closure**
- **Larynx elevation** – Lie on the back, head elevation, shoulders on the floor, looking on toes. The isometric part consists of an alternation of 60 seconds holding an elevated head and 60 seconds rest. The isotonic part consists of 30 seconds of gradual head elevation.

1. Direct treatment
Training of swallowing with food focused on safer food intake orally. These include postural techniques (changes in body position, head during swallowing to facilitate the movement of the bite, change in the direction of movement of the bite, and modification of laryngeal size), compensatory maneuvers (protects airways from aspiration), dietary (consistency adjustment food). During eating, the patient must be alert, attentive, have stable body stability, be in an elevated position.

Training of muscle strength
- Strengthens of tongue muscles.
- Pharynx strengthens (thermo-tactile stimulation and invocation of pharyngeal swallowing phase)
- Improvement of retraction and strength of tongue radix
- Mendelson´s maneuver strengthens laryngo-hyoideum complex elevators and prolongs the time of opening of the upper pharyngeal closure. This reduces residuum in the hypopharynx.
- Super-supraglottic swallow.

Training of structures coordination used by swallowing
- Supraglottic swallow (to close the entrance to the larynx before swallowing)
- Super-supraglottic swallow (maneuver causes collapse of laryngeal vestibulum by the movement of tongue radix to arytenoid cartilage)
- Swallowing and respiration coordination (helps maximal supraglottic pressure during swallowing by breath-holding)
- Bolus holding (helps better timing of oral and pharyngeal phase)

Posture and position
- Head-turning to defected side (reduction of hypopharyngeal residuum)
- Head pronation (prevent aspiration and improve pharyngeal transit)
- Maneuvers combination
- Swallow in the horizontal position on the side (could reduce pharyngeal residuum)

Speech sound disorders

The American Speech-Language-Hearing Association (ASHA), since 2005 use the term Speech Sound Disorders for *articulation disorders* and *phonological disorders*. Symptoms of phonetic and phonologic language levels could occur in various combinations. Reasons for speech sound disorders could be organic and functional.

Organic	functional
Anomalies of articulation organs, defects of teeth and bite occlusion, ankyloglossia	Myofunctional disorder(distortion of sibilants, interdental sigmatism) Orofacial dysfunctions (orofacial muscular disbalance, a disorder of swallowing and respiration, compensatory use of other muscle groups, what deforms upper jaw and makes orthodontic deviations)
Adenoid vegetation (mouth breathing changes the resting position of the tongue)	Iatrogenic reason

Non-specific inheritance	Global motor clumsiness
	Wrong attitude of surrounding to speech and language development

ARTICULATION DISORDERS

relate to the level of specific articulation-motor realizations. The pronunciation of a particular sound does not correspond to the expected pronunciation standard of the native language, but it is recognizable which sound the person pronounces. The sound is formed in another place or in another way, or the person cannot pronounce it at all.

a) in the case of a mental disorder - a symptom of a regressive form of behavior
b) in terms of context: phonetic/contextual – could pronounce the isolated sound but does not use it
c) in terms of disruption: mono form / polyform - in one / more articulation circuits

At the phonetic level, evaluate correct and incorrect pronunciation, phonetic repertoire. The correct pronunciation is the pronunciation of sounds according to a codified language standard. Incorrect pronunciation is a physiological developmental deviation from a codified standard. It is caused by the child's acoustic and motor immaturity. The mechanism of sound formation is not stable. It manifests itself by inaccurate differentiation of sounds, omitting them, or replacing them with an articulatory simpler one. Spontaneous correction can be expected by the child's fifth year.

Mispronunciation differs from a codified standard acoustically or aesthetically, regardless of age. A person makes a sound in the wrong place or in the wrong way. It is called distortion. It is considered the persistence of incorrect articulation after the age of seven as pathological.

PHONOLOGICAL DISORDER

Genetic	• High incidence of developmental learning disabilities in a direct family relative • Below-average performance in language skills tests • Below-average scores in nonsense word repetition tasks • The deficient percentage of distorted sounds • Often in combination with impaired expressive language skills • Good prognosis of correction in the sound plane of speech
Otitis media	• The problem with auditory-cognitive discrimination of phonemes and subsequently with the production of sound • Six or more episodes of otitis at an early age • Decreased speech intelligibility in relation to age • High incidence of pathological phonetic processes (shifting fricatives backward, glottal and nasal substitutions, the omission of the initial consonant • Concurrent occurrence of language impairment • The prognosis of speech adjustment is questionable
Attention, adaptation, cooperation, behavioral deficits,	• Delayed speech development for at least a year • Impaired language skills common • Long-term speech correction prognosis

During development, the child does not always pronounce the same word in the same way (inconsistent pronunciation), which causes reduced speech intelligibility. At the end of the second year, the pronunciation stabilizes.

The current breakdown of phonological processes is:
- physiological phonological development (only physiological phonological processes for a given age)
- delayed phonological development (at least two developmentally younger phonological processes)
- consistent phonological disorder (at the same time developmentally younger and pathological phonological processes occur).

Physiological phonological processes are used by the child in mastering the rules of pronunciation. They are divided into:
- changing the structure of the word
- assimilation
- changing segments of words, the process of substitution, the replacement will require a change in the place/manner of articulation

Developmentally, we divide phonological processes into:
- *early* - they are lost until the 3rd year: omitting an unstressed syllable, omitting a final consonant, moving velar sounds forward
- *late* - simplification of consonant groups, sliding of liquids, closing, replacement of narrowing voices by closing ones

Disruption of the speech sound in childhood is one of the most frequent impairments of communication skills.

Indicative assessment of speech intelligibility in a conversation. Evaluate the number of words that a stranger understands in a conversation with a child. If intelligibility is reduced, it indicates a delay in the development or disturbance of the speech sound, and it does not exhibit distortion. Another option for assessing speech intelligibility is to use the Intelligibility in Context Scale (ICS) by McLeod and his team.

Diagnostics of speech sound disorders

Diagnosis of the phonetic approach
The aim is to determine the child's phonetic repertoire with an emphasis on the identification of absent phonemes and distortion phonemes, diagnose the quality of auditory phoneme differentiation, and the percentage of unspoken consonants and vocals, the level of oromotor skills as a basis for inducing correct articulation.

The child is not born with a knowledge of the sound system of his native language.

Gradually acquires the sounds by imitation. The sound management process is challenging for the child. If he cannot utter a sound, he continually omits it while inserting a particular sound or replacing a sound with another, less demanding one. Constancy is a sign of physiological development.

Diagnostics in phonological approach
The aim is to identify which phonological processes the child uses and to assess whether they are age-appropriate (physiological), age-inappropriate, or pathological phonological processes. We watch the production of each sound at the beginning, middle, and end of the word.

The child uses physiological phonological processes in mastering the rules of pronunciation. They are divided into:

- changing the structure of the word
- assimilation
- changing segments of words, the process of substitution, the replacement will require a change in the place/manner of articulation

Developmentally, can divide phonological processes into:
- early (lost until the 3rd year): omitting an unstressed syllable, omitting a final consonant, moving velar sounds forward
- late: simplification of consonant groups, sliding of liquids, closing, replacement of narrowing sounds by closing ones.

Symptoms in phonetic and phonologic language level:

Articulation deficit	Phonological deficit
Substitution – difficult target vowel replaced with more comfortable sound	Substitution – groups of sounds by sounds which occurs in development later
Omission – of the target sound	Omission –of the target sound, which has a child in phonetic inventory already, mostly at the end of words
Distorsion – wrong pronunciation of target sound	Addition – sounds to the target word, mostly at the end of syllables or word

Therapy of speech sound disorders

The aim is to restore the child's sound system and the acceptable use of sound language in speech production ". Therapy should be designed to respect the specifics of the development and the standard of the language. It is more time-consuming for adolescents and adults. It is a correction of already automated speech stereotypes. Therapeutic procedures should be symptomatic. The aim is to develop the child's sound system and use the sounds according to the relevant language standards.

Approaches are phonetically and phonologically oriented.

Phonetical approach - focused therapy at the motor level aims to master the sound's correct motor implementation, development of the oromotor area, auditory perception, and articulation. It is essential to develop phonematic differentiation (phonematic awareness and analyses).

1. Derivation of new sound:
   - From the view of development
   - Probability of success

- Articulatory continuity
- Nondevelopmental direction
2. Fixation of sound
3. Automatisation of sound
4. Transfer the sound to spontaneous speech

Phonologically focused therapy at the cognitive-linguistic level aims to influence the child's phonological system and induce a systemic change that will affect not only the rehearsed sound.

Principles in the application of phonological therapy:
- systematic planning, detailed analysis of speech production
- constant change in the properties of sounds in the foreground, not the practice of individual sounds
- extension of sound contrasts
- active participation of the child in therapy, right stimulation for activity and preparation of aids according to the criteria of a speech therapist (Marková, J., Gúthová, M., 2005).

Methods:
1. Method of minimal pairs/contrasts
2. Cyclic phonological training
3. Metaphon (Howell, Dean)
4. Parents and children together (Bowen)

The child's articulation should be adjusted before entering primary school, but not later than the end of the first year. "

Cleft palate speech
Sound and resonance of speech depend on the function of velopharyngeal closure, space of nasal and oral cavity, the tongue's position, airflow intensity, air pressure in subglottal, glottal, and supraglottal structures (oropharynx, nasopharynx).
Pathological change of nasality:

Hypernasality (rhinolalia aperta) when the pronunciation of sounds connects oral and nasal cavity, the airflow goes to the mouth instead of the nose.

Causes :

a) Organic:

1. congenital (cleft palate, shortened or non-developed soft palate, deep megapharynx

2. acquired (oronasal communication, neurological diseases, central paresis, peripheral paresis, pseudobulbar paresis)

b) Functional (lower muscle activity of velopharyngeal closure, in hysteria and neurosis, mental retardation, careless speaking style, in deaf people without auditive feedback, as habituation)

Hyponasality (rhinolalia clausa) when airflow goes to the mouth instead of the nose.

Causes:

a) organic:

1. acquired (swelling nasal mucous, hyperplasia nasal shells, rhinitis, tumors, cysts, polyps, hypertrophic tonsils, hudge Passavant´s mound, big adenoids, deformation of nasal septum)

2. congenital(thin nasal ways in deformations of the face, deviated nasal septum)

b) functional (mostly functional defects of velopharyngeal closure muscles)

Mixed rhinolalia occurs by insufficient velopharyngeal mechanism and barrier in nasal and nasopharyngeal cavity.

Palatolalia cleft palate speech

Palatolalia (cleft palate speech) is an impaired communication ability that arises as a secondary consequence of cleft lip and palate. In cleft palate speech, the phonetic-phonological level of speech is primarily disturbed. This can manifest itself as a disorder of nasal resonance and a condition of pronunciation with typical symptoms such as compensatory and palatal articulation.

In severe forms of velopharyngeal insufficiency, can be sometimes observed voice disorders. Some children with a cleft palate may have delayed or impaired speech development (symptoms also at the morphological-syntactic, lexical-semantic, and pragmatic levels of language). Impaired communication skills in palatolalia can be observed in verbal and non-verbal components (in the form of impaired coverbal behavior).

Children with cleft palate do not have more severe forms of swallowing disorders. Only at an early age before palate change, they have difficulty feeding because their palate is not yet completed and cannot separate the oral and nasal cavity. Therefore, the baby cannot create pressure in the mouth and suck milk from the breast and a regular bottle.

Feeding disorders in children with a cleft palate could occur if mothers are without guidance and counseling – can be accompanied by low nutritional intake, slow weight gain, nasal regurgitation and "swallowing air" during feeding, which can cause colic in the baby, restlessness and frequent crying and emotional stress in mothers.

If more severe feeding problems persist after the operation, could be neurological cause or anomalies associated with the syndromes.

Diagnostics of cleft palate speech

The speech therapist should pay special attention to the evaluation of the velopharyngeal mechanism function with diagnostic therapy. The results are an essential source of information for the cleft team and determine the child's next course of treatment - deciding on the secondary palatal surgery (pharyngeal lobe).

The essence of diagnostic therapy is that the clinical speech therapist can assess whether the child's velopharyngeal mechanism is sufficient for normal speech after a specific section of articulatory training. More precisely, he can evaluate whether the child can learn to articulate consonants correctly requiring pressure.

Symptoms of articulation disorder associated with velopharyngeal mechanism function, especially weakened articulation, together with the symptoms of hypernasality, serve in diagnostic therapy as a guide.

Weak articulation is within the triad of velopharyngeal insufficiency characters, a safe indicator of velopharyngeal mechanism insufficiency in children with no other anatomical defects.

The triad of velopharyngeal insufficiency:
- attenuated pressure of oral sounds formed on correct articulation sites,
- consistent nasal emissions and
- hypernasality.

Suppose a speech therapist in a child maps to weak articulation and triad of Velopharyngeal insufficiency (VPI) characters, before speech therapy or after performing a certain section articulation therapy (during the removal of compensatory sounds). In that case, the child shall be sent immediately to the cleft counseling of these symptoms with suspected VPI and a recommendation to secondary surgery.

Symptoms of cleft palate speech

	Specific symptoms		Associated symptoms	Parallel symptoms of speech disorder unrelated to cleft palate
Articulation deficits	Resonance deficits	Other symptoms of velopharyngeal insufficiency		
-Compensatory -Weak -Palatal -Velar -Dental	-Hypernasality -Hyponasality -Mixed nasality -Cul de Sac resonance	-Weak sounds -Pressure -Nasal emissions -Co movements of the nose and lobe	-delayed speech and language development -phonological deficits -palatophonia	-articulation disorder -language skill deficits

The scale of speech intelligibility by Kerekrétyová:
1. Good 2. Socially acceptable 3. Worse 4. Incomprehensible

Classification of velopharyngeal mechanism function	
The function of the velopharyngeal mechanism	symptomatology
Sufficient	Produce at least some oral consonants which need pressure (P,B,F,V,T,D...) regular at right places, without failure of pressure, without nasal emissions; normal resonance
Insufficient	Produce at least some oral consonants which need pressure weak on the right places, but with failure of pressure, with nasal emissions, and hypernasality
border	Produce only a few oral consonants which need pressure weak, and some produced properly, sometimes could be border failure of pressure, nasal border emissions, and border hypernasality

Impossible assesment	With compensatory extraoral sounds, omitted all oral consonants which need pressure
Impossible assesment	With another anatomical defect, extensive oronasal and vestibulonasal communications with complete inability of bilabial closure

Basic evaluation:

- Gutzman´s A-I test (differential diagnostic hypo and hypernasality)
- Czermak´s test (mirror misting up by sounds pronunciation – hypernasality)
- Test with otophon (hypernasality)
- Schlessinger´s test (differs organic and functional hypernasality, change to worse in standing position than in horisontal.
- Test of inflation of cheeks (sufficiency of velopharyngeal mechanism)
- Nadoleczny´s test of turning head (by turning head to saved side hypernasality rises, to the impaired side it decreases)
- Arnold´s diagnostic rule (nose breathing is difficult only by organic hyponasality)
- Manometric test
- Spirometric test
- Test of the soft palate with reflectoric gagging
- *Instrumental tests:* videofluoroscopic evaluation, endoscopy, *fibroscopy,* electromyography, *s*onographic analyses, aerodynamic analyses
- *Diagnostic based on acoustic analyses and subjective evaluation:* word and pictures tests, articulation tests, *an* inspection of the oral and nasal cavity

Therapy of cleft palate speech

The treatment of a child with cleft palate is multidisciplinary and can be divided into medical and non-medical ingredients. Some medical treatment steps are aimed directly at or indirectly at speech (cleft operations, oronasal communication closing, bite correction, velopharyngeal insufficiency operation, correction nasal septum, etc.). The speech therapist needs to be informed to be able to do plan therapy correctly. Therefore, it is necessary that the cleft clinic, its experts, and a speech therapist who has the child in continuous care work closely together.

Speech and language therapy treatment are non-medical, conservative, or in other words, behavioral, non-pharmacological therapy. The term behavioral, non-pharmacological therapy covers all speech therapy methods, but it is used very ambiguously and also refers to such approaches, which are ineffective or contraindicated.

Adequate clinical and speech therapy for children with cleft palate has two main components:
1. articulation training
2. early phoneme stimulation in the first words.

Other valuable areas of therapy are stimulation language and phonological skills and voice therapy. Treatment focused on velopharyngeal mechanism function and resonance is controversial, some completely ineffective and contraindicated. The goal is to eliminate the symptoms of palatolalia and practicing the child's normal speech. However, in some children with severe clefts, this is not always possible during treatment, and then we try to alleviate the symptoms as much as possible.

Methods of speech and language therapy

Goals of therapy	Methods
Early intervention (0-36 month)	
Advice after birth, before cleft palate operation (0-12month)	Advice, talk, leaflets about the cleft palate, therapy, child development, speech, and language development
Early intervention (12-36 month) Teach parents communication strategies and special technics	Communication strategies training and methods for mother in systematic therapies
Preschool age (3-7 years, sometimes later)	
Articulation training	
Removal of compensatory articulation Removal of vowel speech According to the course of symptoms removal, determine whether is the velopharyngeal mechanism functional	Specific technic of sounds derivation The direction of articulation airflow Multimodal monitoring of correct and incorrect articulation, negative training Specific phonological awareness Elimination of coarticulation Intensive training of parents as co-therapeuts Syllable, word, sentence drill therapy Systematic and intensive training of pronunciation
Weak articulation: evaluation severity and advice of surgery therapy	Evaluation of triade velopharyngeal insufficiency signs and severity Evaluation of other anatomical defects Send the child to cleft palate counseling to consider surgery Advice to parents

Removal palatal articulation Removal velar articulation	Specific derivation of alveolar sounds by anteriorisation Multimodal monitoring of correct and incorrect articulation, negative training Elimination of coarticulation Specific phonological awareness Syllable, word, sentence drill therapy Systematic and intensive training of pronunciation
Removal dental articulation	Monitoring of orthodontic therapy and synchronization with articulation training Test of stimulability Systematic pronunciation training
Removal of dyslalic (incorrect) articulation	In specific articulation training
Removal of resonance defects	
Removal of hyper and hyponasality	Speech and language therapy is almost always ineffective Surgery
Phonological therapy	
Ability self-differentiation of incorrect articulation Stimulation of phonological awareness	Multimodal monitoring of correct and incorrect articulation, negative training Specific phonological awareness
Stimulation of language abilities	
Symptoms of severe incomprehensibility as the cause of developmental language disorder Removal symptoms of developmental language disorder	Removal of severe speech incomprehensibility Articulation training Removal of developmental disorder
Voice disorders	
Removal of velopharyngeal insufficiency symptoms and compensatory articulation as the cause of voice disorder Removal of voice disorders	Surgery Removal of compensatory sounds by articulation therapy Voice therapy
Blowing and other nonspeech technics	
Strengthens of palate muscles	Forced blowing, yawning, gargling, irritation with cotton sticks, palate massages, sucking movements
Resonance training	
Removal or masking symptoms of hypernasality	Resonance training with audio feedback Making bigger jaw angle Manipulation of speech intensity Smooth articulation contacts Hard articulation contacts Making slower speech pace

Removal of hypernasality and developmental language disorder symptoms with instrumental biofeedback	Nasometer Continuous Positive Airway Pressure device (CPAP)
Speech prosthesis	
Velopharyngeal insufficiency prothesis obturation or elevating off the immobile palate Stimulation movements of the velopharyngeal mechanism by reduction of prothesis	Speech bullet Palatal elevator

Specific learning disabilities

The difficulties manifest at the beginning of schooling. Children with learning disabilities find it challenging to learn through conventional teaching methods, although they have adequate intelligence and a sufficiently stimulating family environment. The consequences of learning disabilities (frustration, traumatization, depression, behavioral problems caused by constant school failures) are often more severe problems than the disorders themselves. They negatively affect the personal, social, educational, and professional development of these children.

Therefore, it is necessary to promptly capture children with learning disabilities, individual approach, positive motivation, correct techniques and methods of work, and reeducation-therapeutic care.

Many children with communication deficits, especially children with developmental language disorder (specifically impaired speech development / developmental dysphasia / developmental language disorder) show a specific learning disability in school age. In contrast, particular learning disabilities are often a natural continuation of the language deficits.

Dyslexia (reading disorder) - The condition affects the speed, technique, accuracy of reading, and comprehension of the text.

Manifestations of dyslexia:
- difficulties in recognizing individual letters (connected letter - sound), the problem of remembering and memorizing personal letters
- replacement of shape-like letters (b-d-p, m-n, u-n, z-s, k-h, a-e)
- replacement of letters whose sounds are acoustically similar (ž-š, h-ch, b-p, z-s, k-g, t-d, ť-ď ...)
- replacement of functionally similar letters (vowels a-e-o-u, consonants h-k-l)

- omitting letters in words, words in sentences
- non-respect of the number of vowels
- the inability to read with intonation
- incorrect reading of prepositional phrases
- difficulties in connecting sounds into syllables, syllables into words
- difficulties in transitioning from syllable to fluent reading
- often, there is "Double reading" (silent reading of words)
- guessing the ending of a word according to the correctly read beginning
- difficulty reading the words in which the consonant group occurs
- word distortion, or inserting letters into words that do not happen there
- problems in observing punctuation marks - non-respect of dots, question marks, lengths
- no distinction between soft and hard syllables - weak syllables read hard and another way round
- after reading, often the inability to reproduce and say in your own words the content of the text
- shallow breathing while reading - tension

Dysgraphia (writing disorder) - is a reduced ability to inability to acquire writing skills. Affects the graphic (formal side) of the written expression, not the content. Difficulties manifest themselves in mastering font shapes, in imitating and memorizing them. The handwriting of a child with dysgraphia is immature to illegible.

Manifestations of dysgraphia:
- noncompliance with the size and shape of letters
- incorrect font spacing
- a child with dysgraphia does not remember the shape of the letter; he cannot imitate it
- mirrored shapes of letters
- does not follow the line (writes below the line, above the line ...)
- disproportionately slow writing pace
- writing clumsy
- lines and strokes sharp, incoherent
- increased pressure on the pad
- incorrect pen grip
- the student often strikes, rewrites the letters
- the font is difficult to read
- replaces similar letters (m/n, b/d, h/k/l, z/s, a/o, t/d ...)

Dysortography (spelling disorder) - Children with dysorthography have a weaker language feeling, which is subsequently reflected in difficulties in applying learned spelling rules.

Manifestations of dysorthography:
- difficulties in discriminating soft and hard syllables dy/di, ty/ti, ny/ni, ly/li (Slovak language)
- writing syllable di, ti, ni, li, de, te, ne, le with soft (Slovak language)
- problematic discrimination of short and long vowels (Slovak language)
- disrespecting the order of letters in words, omitting letters, shifting the order of letters in words, inserting vowels into consonant groups, adding letters
- unmanaged sentence analysis, the indistinguishability of sentence boundaries, concatenation of words in sentences.

Dyscalculia (impaired mathematical abilities) - this is a significantly disturbed structure of currencies for mathematics at the standard level and general intelligence structure, except for the mathematical factor. Dyscalculia means lagging in understanding mathematical concepts, relationships and applying them in solving mathematical problems.

Manifestations of dyscalculia:

Practicognostic dyscalculia
- unable adequate mathematically to manipulate specific or drawn symbols (formation of groups according to some common feature, colors, sizes, shapes), difficulty sorting objects by color, size, shape, length
- cannot compare groups by the number
- cannot estimate the number of items without deduction
- difficulties in differentiating geometric shapes

Verbal dyscalculia
- difficulty in verbally marking quantities, numbers of objects, numbers, operating characters, or arithmetic acts
- cannot show the verbally stated number of fingers, objects
- cannot name a series of numbers in the ascending and descending direction, multiples of numbers, even and odd numbers

Lexical dyscalculia
- cannot read mathematical symbols (numbers, operating characters)

- replaces operational symbols (+ for -,. for:)
- not able to read multi-digit numbers with zeros, numbers written vertically
- replaces similar numbers (6/9, 3/8), Roman numerals (VI/IV), number 561 reads as 5, 6, 1

Graphic dyscalculia
- cannot write mathematical characters, numbers ...
- difficulty in writing multi-digit numbers (writes them in reverse order, forgets to write zeros)
- writes disproportionately large numbers, written speech is untidy
- when writing under oneself, the student is not able to place units under units, tens under tens
- drawing problems appear in geometry

Operational dyscalculia
- not able to perform mathematical operations - addition, subtraction, multiplication, division
- often confusions in mathematical operations
- do written counting of such examples that can be easily mastered by memory
- difficulty solving combined tasks, where it is necessary to keep in mind the individual results of the so-called chain 5 + 3 + 8-2

Ideognostic dyscalculia
- problems in conceptual activity, in the understanding of mathematical concepts and relationships between them
- problems in the number series (counting by two, by five, etc.)
- number 6 can read and write but does not understand that 6 is 2.3, 3 + 3, 10-4
- difficulties are manifested in word tasks (not able to transfer the practical problem into the system of numbers and solve it)

Diagnostics of specific learning disabilities

Diagnostics of reading skills
Reading exams for younger school age - the test consists of three separate exams:
1. Text reading;
2. Word reading;
3. Reading the pseudology.

The tests make it possible to analyze and compare the speed and accuracy of reading words and pseudo-language, reading technique, comprehension of the read text, understanding of the meaning of the read text, and reading errors.

Word-reading reading test - a normative test of silent reading comprehension. The speed and accuracy of reading and the level of understanding are evaluated and compared with the standard. It is diagnostically very interesting to compare the student's results in testing loud reading (e.g. the above test) and the results in this test.

Diagnosis of spelling skills

Assessment of spelling skills in younger students - is a comprehensive set of spelling tests focused on different levels of application of spelling rules in the Slovak language, from the phonemic principle to the application of complex regulations in written word notation. A significant benefit is the ability to quantitatively and qualitatively analyze errors in individual subtests, allowing better identification of problem areas.

Evaluation of spelling skills in older students - a test consisting of writing 50 dictated words dictated to the test subject in phrases and a specific spelling phenomenon, and a total number of non-specific errors are observed. The test is simple to administer and evaluate but practically focuses on higher spelling levels and is not sensitive enough to fundamental mistakes in applying the phonemic principle. The test authors recommend supplementing the results with a qualitative analysis of school dictations, notebooks, and stylistic works (Mikulajová et al., 2012).

Diagnostics of mathematical abilities

Tests can be divided into:
- **Complex:** Word problems, Mathematical advice, Analogies, Numerical autodictation, Numerical operations, Perceptual-numerical test form A, Perceptual-numerical test form B, Laterality test
- **Perceptual-motor:** Directional Orientation, Rey-Osterrieth complex figure
- **Perceptual-cognitive:** Visual differentiation, Number structure
- **Verbal:** Meaning of mathematical terms.

Diagnostics of writing and graphomotor skills

Diagnosis of the graphic expression level is carried out exclusively by qualitative analysis of written expression - dictation, transcription, depreciation, or autodictate.

The final graphic notation's basic attributes are observed in the visual expression: inclination, size, shape, and relation of the grapheme and adherence to the lineature. The tempo and fluency of writing, grip of the typeface, movements of the wrist, elbow, shoulder joint, and position when writing are evaluated from the writing process.

In the diagnosis of developmental coordination disorder, formerly referred to as dysgraphia, it is necessary to respect the specifics of a student's development - levels of fine motor skills, visual-motor coordination, and other physical and mental areas development of the child concerning the environment. A fundamental criterion in determining a developmental coordination disorder is the degree of discrepancy between different academic abilities and writing. The determining factor in diagnostics is to exclude the influence of organ damage.

Specific learning disabilities comorbidities commonly occur in conjunction with another neurodevelopmental disorder, Attention Disorder and Hyperactivity Deficit, communication disorder, developmental motor coordination disorder, autism spectrum disorder or other mental disorder, anxiety disorder, depressive or bipolar disorder.

These comorbidities make examination and differential diagnosis difficult, and the cooperation of several experts (speech therapist, child psychiatrist, neurologist, clinical psychologist) is necessary.

Only one source of data is not enough to diagnose. The diagnosis should be based on a summary of anamnestic data (health, developmental, school, family), based on a history of learning difficulties including past and present manifestations, documentation of the effects of problems on school, work, or social life based on past and current school reports, summaries of evaluations from the school, curriculum vitae and based on past and current results of individual standardized tests or school performance. Because a specific learning disability typically persists into adulthood, re-evaluations are usually unnecessary unless there are some significant changes (improvement or deterioration) or an examination is required for specific purposes.

Therapy of specific learning disabilities

There are two different methodological procedures:

- Training of partial capabilities
- Learning strategies (strategy of illustrative modeling)

Stimulation of underdeveloped functions needed for the formation of reading and writing ability:

- Auditive perception
- Phonematic awareness
- Visual perception
- Spatial and left-right orientation
- Speech
- Psychic processes

While there is no cure for a specific learning disorder, there are many ways to improve reading, writing, and math skills for a child. Treatment usually includes strengthening the skills and developing a learning strategy tailored to take advantage of a child's strengths. For example, repetition and mnemonic devices might make it easier to memorize a math formula, and drawing a picture to illustrate a word problem might help a child visualize what is being asked.

Treatment for specific learning disorders often also involves multimodal teaching. If a child has trouble comprehending a subject with his or her eyes and ears alone, other senses such as touch, taste, and even smell can play a role in the learning process.

A learning specialist can help determine the services or accommodations a child might benefit from at school. Psychotherapy, cognitive behavior therapy, in particular, may also help treat the emotional and behavioral problems that can accompany specific learning disorders.

Students receive most of their education in a general education classroom, with direct or indirect support from special education professionals. However, part-time or full-time placement in a special education classroom or even placement in a special school may be necessary for some students.

Voice disorders

Dysphonia - voice disorder or aphonia - complete loss of voice is an impaired communication ability in children and adults.

The voice is a basic precondition for sounded spoken speech. It is not only the oldest but also the first means of communication of a person from birth. It is an integral part of every individual we do not realize until we lose it. "The voice is a direct expression of the soul" (Alfred Wolfsohn).

Etiological classification

- structural changes on vocal cords (laryngitis, vocal nodules, hemorrhagic, edema, carcinoma, hyperkeratosis, granuloma, cyst, leukoplakia, papilloma)
- neurogenic voice disorders (paresis, spasm, essential tremor, by neurological diseases like myasthenia gravis, ALS, Parkinson´s syndrome)
- systematic diseases (diseases of pulmonary system, infectious diseases, Gastroesophageal reflux (GER), allergy, diseases of immunity system)
- behaviorally conditioned (overusing of voice, pressed phonation, voice fatigue, incorrect use of voice, pubertophonia, ventricular phonation)
- idiopathic (congenital anomalies of pulmonary system, stenosis, laryngomalacia, paradox movements of vocal cords)

Diagnostics of voice disorders

Diagnostics is based on a medical (ENT, phoniatric) examination, which evaluates phonation organs condition with aspexia (observation), laryngoscopy or videostroboscopy.

The clinical speech therapy examination itself includes:

1. establishing contact
2. anamnestic-diagnostic interview (family history, abuse, bad habits, emotional state, subjective evaluation)
3. tactile assessment of musculoskeletal tone and body posture
4. voice evaluation of the following voice parameters:
    - o   vocal onset (soft-hard-breathableň
    - o   voice quality (sharp, bold, hoarse, monotonous or bizarre intonation, sudden voice pauses and breaks, diplophony, tremor, inspirational phonation, fatigue)
    - o   voice position (decreased, increased, variable, fistulous voiceň
    - o   voice intensity (micro / - macrophony, variable)
5. resonance (hypo / -hypernasality)
6. speed of speech (tachy / -bradylalia)
7. phonation time (phonation vocals A and I quietly and loudly, index S / Z)
8. respiration - dyspnoea (exertion, stridor, shallow, bone, abdominal breathing)

Kerekrétiová recommends the use of the following diagnostic methods within the special clinical-speech therapy examination of voice disorders:

- evaluation of continuous conversational speech (acoustic-perceptual evaluation of all voice parameters, phonation, respiration, articulation)

- reading standard text(acoustic-perceptual evaluation of all voice parameters, phonation, respiration, articulation)
- counting -automatism (acoustic-perceptual evaluation of all voice parameters, phonation, respiration, articulation)
- repeating of sentences of words with vowels on the beginning (acoustic-perceptual evaluation of all voice parameters, phonation, respiration, articulation)
- prolonged phonation „A,S,Z" (acoustic-perceptual evaluation of all voice parameters, phonation, respiration, articulation)
- singing or „sirene" on the scale (frequency rate)
- „uhm" test (optimal position of voice)
- „hej" test (dynamic voice rate)
- Gutzman´s A-I test (resonance)

The most common and primary symptom of voice disorders is a change in the original voice parameters. There are eight primary symptoms of pathological phonation:

1. snoring
2. vocal fatigue - occurs mainly after long speaking and singing. However, depending on the patient's overall health and condition, especially in his general weakness, it can manifest even after a short time.
3. voice with a whisper - is a consequence of voice insufficiency. It also manifests itself as an inability to say the whole sentence without replenishing the air with a new touch.
4. decreased vocal range - appears at the beginning only during singing, there are problems with singing the upper tones of the vocal frequency range for fatigue and pain.
5. aphonia - can appear gradually or suddenly. The patient uses a whisper because he has "lost" his voice, feels dry in his throat, and every attempt to create a voice is associated with significant effort
6. fractures in height/force - these are sudden, unexpected changes, as lost control of the voice, the position of the voice changes irregularly, jumps to the fistula voice, which is typical of mutations
7. voice formed with tension - arises due to a disorder of the musculoskeletal system. The patient complains of a "constricted throat," a foreign body feeling, problems with starting and maintaining phonation, lack of stability.
8. tremor - a typical shaky and weak voice. The patient cannot keep the voice at one level, at the same height and strength.

Other symptoms of voice disorders include diplophonia - two voices. At pathological intensity, a microphone appears - low voice intensity or microphony - strong voice to scream.

Therapy of voice disorders

The therapy of voice disorders requires the cooperation of a professional team of various medical disciplines (EarNoseThroat, phonics, phonosurgeon, pulmonologist, psychiatrist, neurologist, balneologist), clinical speech-language therapists, clinical psychologists as well as physiotherapists.

In therapy removes, alleviates, or stabilizes voice disorders, streamlines the comprehensibility of verbal communication, or in very severe and progressive diseases, offers to improve overall communication, the ability of alternative or augmentative communication options.

Medical disciplines provide phonosurgical solutions, drug, inhalation, and balneotherapy, equipping patients with voice prostheses and voice cannulas: clinical psychologists, psychotherapy and relaxation methodologies, physiotherapists, breathing gymnastics, therapeutic physical education.

The main content of clinical-speech therapy intervention within voice reeducation is phonation therapy. It is based on an individual reeducation plan that focuses on proper posture, the practice of proper breathing with a predominance of abdominal breathing, and the acquisition of physiological voice production. Before starting the therapy, however, it is necessary to get the patient for active cooperation. An integral part of the treatment is also voice calm and patient education about voice hygiene.

Voice exercises
- extension of phonation time,
- improving voice resonance,
- soft voice beginnings,
- optimal middle voice position,
- diaphragm support.
- punching voice exercises and vocal cord closure exercises hypofunctional techniques in vocal cord insufficiency in hypotension and vocal cord paresis,
- relaxing nasalized voice exercises, so-called hyper-functional techniques in hyperkinetic dysphonia, and printed phonation aimed at releasing increased laryngeal tension,

- training of substitute voice mechanisms of pseudo-whisper, esophageal voice after total laryngectomy
- -technique of reducing high voice (hard glottal attack) by a method of very hard vocal beginnings
- -non-verbal communication using alternative and augmentative communication (pictograms, sounded PC programs based on writing) in aphonia, or during the "voice holidays."

In case of repeated recurrence of dysphonia or its resistance to clinical-speech therapy intervention, spa treatment based on the recommendation and indication of a specialist doctor is appropriate.